FORMULA F

Mouth Power
+ Word Power

Personal Power

We are living in an age of the "quick fix." Some people want everything *now* without expending any effort or accepting any personal responsibility. They want someone else to take care of things for them. Unfortunately, these people are doomed to great disappointment and non-achievement.

We achieve success in life when we accept responsibility for ourselves and are willing to do whatever it takes, including being patient, to achieve our goals. Someone else can teach us how, or give us proven formulas for success, but in the final analysis we must do it ourselves. This is the way life is.

The self-talk techniques put forth in this book *do* fit in with the "quick fix" philosophy—they are fast and easy to execute and do, in fact, bring quick results. The big difference is that this book teaches you to be fully in charge of your own destiny, to accept personal responsibility for yourself and execute your responsibilities in such a way as to ensure your ultimate success.

For those of you who want to take charge of your own lives, *The Art of Self Talk* gives you the tools to do just that. It will be your winning formula every time.

About the Author

William Hewitt has devoted most of his adult life to training, teaching, motivating, and counseling people. This book is his sixth in a series of self-help, how-to books. He lectures and conducts workshops on personal development, and as a certified hypnotherapist, as well as a professional astrologer, has counseled and guided hundreds of people to capitalize on their strengths, overcome problems, and create better lives for themselves. A former IBM executive and non-commissioned air force officer, he now spends his time writing both for the public and for private industry.

To Write to the Author

If you wish to contact the author or would like more information about this book, please write to the author in care of Llewellyn Worldwide, and we will forward your request. Both the author and publisher appreciate hearing from you and learning of your enjoyment of this book and how it has helped you. Llewellyn Worldwide cannot guarantee that every letter written to the author can be answered, but all will be forwarded. Please write to:

William W. Hewitt
c/o Llewellyn Worldwide
P.O. Box 64383-334, St. Paul, MN 55164-0383, U.S.A.
Please enclose a self-addressed, stamped envelope for reply, or $1.00 to cover costs. If outside U.S.A., enclose international postal reply coupon.

Free Catalog from Llewellyn

For more than ninety years Llewellyn has brought its readers knowledge in the fields of metaphysics and human potential. Learn about the newest books in spiritual guidance, natural healing, astrology, occult philosophy and more. Enjoy book reviews, new age articles, a calendar of events, plus current advertised products and services. To get your free copy of *Llewellyn's New Worlds*, send your name and address to:

Llewellyn's New Worlds
P.O. Box 64383-334, St. Paul, MN 55164-0383, U.S.A.

Llewellyn's Self-Improvement Series

The Art of Self Talk

Formula For Success:

Mouth Power + Word Power = Personal Power

William W. Hewitt

1993
Llewellyn Publications
St. Paul, Minnesota 64383-0383, U.S.A.

FIRST EDITION, 1993

Cover Design by Christopher Wells

Library of Congress Cataloging-in-Publication Data
Hewitt, William W., 1929–
    The art of self talk : formula for success / William W. Hewitt
      p.   cm. — (Llewellyn's self-improvement series)
    ISBN 0-87542-334-5
      1. Self talk. 2. Success. I. Title. II. Series.
BF697.5.S47H 1992   92-31657
158'.1—dc20   CIP

Llewellyn Publications
A Division of Llewellyn Worldwide, Ltd.
St. Paul, Minnesota 55164-0383, U.S.A.

About Llewellyn's Self-Improvement Series

We all desire to live a "full life," one that we can look back on with no regrets. Yet many of us live from day to day feeling that "something" in our life is missing, or that we have become a victim of circumstances which make happiness impossible.

Ironically, even when we desire to make a positive change in our life, we often stick with situations or behaviors that are unhealthy for us, be they bad relationships, unfulfilling work, or addictions to food, money, sex, or drugs.

The greatest barrier to human growth is the illusion of helplessness and powerlessness. It is the illusion that we have no choices in life.

Nothing could be further from the truth. Everyone has inherent resources to succeed if he or she learns to tap into them. And that's where self-empowerment comes in.

To empower yourself means to make choices to improve your life with commitment, style and joyfulness. It is reclaiming your own creative power to change, to love and nurture yourself, and to persevere in obtaining your goals. It is ultimately about creating your own reality.

Llewellyn's Self-Improvement Series gives you a direct opportunity to improve yourself and your life through practical, step-by-step guidance from people who have mastered the techniques they share. It challenges you to be the best you can be, to *experience change*, not just read about it. It challenges you to surrender old assumptions and self-deceit in favor of growth and honesty. It challenges you to affect deep and powerful changes in your life.

Congratulations. You have already taken the first, most important step toward reclaiming your own amazing power. You have chosen to read this book. A full and rewarding life is yours for the living.

Other Books by the Author

Hypnosis
Beyond Hypnosis
Tea Leaf Reading
Astrology for Beginners
Bridges to Success and Fulfillment

TABLE OF CONTENTS

This book is dedicated to
Carl Llewellyn Weschcke,
my friend and my mentor,
who guided me to become
a successful author.

Chapter 1

The Mouth That Roared

(What Self Talk Is All About)

At some time or the other we have all heard or used the term "all psyched up."

"I psyched myself up for the job interview."

"I knew it would be a difficult task, so I psyched myself up for it."

"I am all psyched up for the exam.

The above statements are the kind of expressions to which I am referring.

But what does "all psyched up" mean in this context? It usually means we have had a little mental pep talk with ourselves with regard to some situation we are concerned about.

You are apprehensive about some event or situation so you tell yourself you will be confident,

1

unafraid, strong, well prepared, in control, mentally alert, and so forth. You are the coach preparing your team for the big game—and you are both the coach and the team.

And the amazing thing is that it *really* works!

But why does it work? What is really going on? Is it magic? Is it self-delusion? Is it coincidence? No, it is none of these things. It is something else entirely. Something so simple, so natural that we don't give it a second thought.

If we did give it a second thought, we would say, "WOW! I really have a great power inside me. I want to learn how to use this power effectively so my entire life will be better. I want to be a winner all the time!"

The purpose of this book is to do just that—to give a second thought to that special force you have locked up within you—to show you how to unlock and unleash that force at will—to show you how to be a winner in life, all the time.

No, this is not another one of those pie-in-the-sky, Pollyanna-type, world-through-rose-colored-glasses books that says a lot of nice things, though you never quite know what to do with them.

This is a nuts and bolts book. This is a gut level book. This book briefly, simply tells you what is going on inside you. Then it gives you many different how-to scenarios from which to choose that you can do to make things happen for you. These are methods you can start doing today. These are methods that are "do-able" within the framework of your current lifestyle, regardless of what your lifestyle is.

You don't have to do all the methods in this book unless you want to. Any one of the methods is okay. You can, of course, perform as many as you wish. I give you a variety to choose from because everyone is unique. What strikes your fancy may be different than what strikes another person's fancy. Whatever best fits you in this book, use. Whatever doesn't fit you, just read for information but don't dwell on. You may want to give everything a try in order to decide what fits best for you.

Some of you are business people, and you want to do a better job and be more successful. Some of you want to do a better job of interacting with other people. Some want to improve their own behavior, be it self-confidence, attitude, memory, etc. Others may be spiritual and want to advance in that area.

Some want to purchase a new automobile without getting a bad deal. Some are supervisors and managers who want to be more effective. Some are workers who want to be able to have a better relationship with their bosses. Parents want to interact better with their spouses and children, and vice versa. We all would like to always be "at the right place at the right time." And who wouldn't like to be a bit more well off financially?

The things you can learn from this book can enable you to successfully deal with these situations or virtually any other situation you choose.

And the neat thing about it is that it is easy, simple, natural, and doable right now. And there is one side effect you get for free—*it is fun.*

Your mouth is a powerful tool, and in the next chapter I will show you how to use your mouth in an unusual and powerful way to bring about astounding changes in your life. I will teach you to become the mouth that roared in a technique called "self talk." I will teach you to talk out loud in a special way in order to program your mind for success.

The spoken word has exceptional power to program the subconscious mind. That is why self talk is such a powerful tool for you to use to shape or reshape your life. Let me cite a true experience I had that illustrates how the spoken word can reprogram your mind.

When I finished my basic training in the Air Force some years ago, I was sent to radar school for technical training. The school was eight hours a day, five days a week, for 40 weeks—a total of 200 days.

Every day the instructor took roll call first thing before class started. Usually there was a different instructor each week, although several instructors did teach more than one week and some only taught a few days here and there.

On the first day, the instructor started the roll call. As he called each last name in alphabetical order, the student would respond with, "Present!"

"Alberts!"

"Present!"

"Bostick!"

"Present!"

And so forth. I knew my name should be called after Gager.

"Gager!"

"Present!"

"Johnson!"

What happened? Why didn't the sergeant call Hewitt? I will tell him when he is finished that they left my name off the roster.

"Newitt!" The instructor called, pronouncing knee-wit. No answer. I looked around the room wondering who knee-wit was. "Newitt!" The instructor called again. Still knee-wit did not answer. "Newitt, William W.!"

The "William W." got my attention, and my mind finally registered that my last name must be incorrectly spelled on the roster.

"Present, Sergeant, but the name is Hewitt, pronounced hew-it, not knee-wit." I spelled it out for him: H E W I T T.

"Typographical error," the sergeant replied. "I'll get it fixed.

The next day was the exact same scenario. I was still Newitt (knee-wit) on the roster, and the instructor vowed to get it fixed.

Every day without exception I was "Newitt." And I always responded mechanically, "Not knee-wit. It is hew-it."

It became a standing joke, and my buddies all started calling me Newitt (knee-wit).

On day 196, we got a brand new instructor fresh out of instructor's training. Again the roster was still incorrect and we went through the usual "Not knee-wit. It is hew-it" scenario with the instructor vowing to get the roster corrected.

On day 197, the roll call went like this: "Gager!" "Present!" "Hewitt!"

"Not Hewitt. It is Newitt!" I responded automatically without thinking.

The class roared with laughter because I had taken on the identity of "Newitt" at a subconscious level and had responded accordingly. I hadn't intended to be funny. It was a conditioned response.

The most powerful and personal identity a person has is their name; and yet, through the spoken word repeated hundreds of times, I had automatically been conditioned to assume another name—Newitt—when I was in the classroom environment. I actually thought of myself as being Newitt (knee-wit).

Now that is both scary and awesome. Scary because you realize that much damage can be done with the spoken word. Awesome because you realize how much good can be done with the spoken word.

This book is all about using the spoken word as a powerful tool for achieving good in your life. With self talk you can enrich every area of your life beyond your wildest imagination.

When you start talking to yourself as prescribed in this book, your life will grow richer in every respect.

In subsequent chapters I will show you how to deal with a variety of everyday situations successfully—from making peace after an argument to getting a good deal when purchasing an automobile.

Formula For Success:
Mouth Power + Word Power = Personal Power

Chapter 2

Want an Intelligent Conversation?

(Then Talk to Yourself)

It used to be that anyone who talked out loud to him/herself was thought to be "not quite right in the head."

People would make gestures like pointing a finger to their temple while making a circular motion with it to indicate the person talking to him/herself was screwed up in the head. They would make snide remarks such as: "He is a dollar short of having fifty cents," or "He doesn't have both oars in the water," or "His pilot light blew out," or some similar remark.

Today things are changing. It is now the smart thing to do to talk out loud to yourself. If you want

9

an intelligent conversation, talk out loud to yourself. If you want constructive change in your life, talk out loud to yourself. Have diarrhea of the mouth, so to speak, and achievement is at your doorstep. It is the smart people, not the unstable ones, who talk out loud to themselves. And there is good reason for this.

Each of us has goals, desires, and needs. Some of these goals are lofty such as becoming famous. Some goals are mundane, such as finding stable employment. And there are an infinite number of goals, desires, and needs in between. The amazing thing is that we all have built within us everything we need to achieve whatever it is we want—if we know how to activate that power we already possess. Most successful people know how to activate that power, either consciously or subconsciously. That is why they are successful.

In this book I will show you how to consciously activate your innate power in concert with your subconscious power to become a dynamo of self-achieving power.

This book is primarily about self talk: Talking out loud to yourself at certain times in a certain way in order to activate your innate power. Each of the subsequent chapters deals with a specific situation and how to use self talk to handle it. A sufficient variety of situations are covered to enable you to devise additional methods for any unique situation you have in mind. You are free to use the methods in this book exactly as written or to alter them to suit yourself. The key element in whatever you do is:

Talk out loud to yourself frequently, with emotion, with confidence, knowing you are programming yourself for the results you desire.

Why does talking out loud to yourself work? To answer this, first let me digress to briefly discuss silent talking and how your subconscious mind works.

We all talk to ourselves mentally about one thing or the other. Most often, it concerns solving some minor daily problem such as balancing the budget, deciding on how to discuss some sensitive subject with another person, or deciding on the best approach in handling a job-related problem, and so forth.

Occasionally, we give ourselves mental pep talks in preparation for a job interview or similar situation.

Less frequently, but more importantly, we have a major problem to handle and we have a silent debate about resolving it. These would be situations such as: saving your marriage from divorce; overcoming a serious health problem; dealing with a child's drug problem, and so forth.

If you are really expert in mental talk, if you have extraordinary powers of concentration, and if your mind is exceptionally well-disciplined, you will achieve the results you want through the use of mental talk. It does work quite well, especially if you combine good visualization during the mental talk.

The common problem with mental self talk is that most people do not have the necessary powers of concentration, or the self-disciplined mind, or the good visualization ability. Lacking any one of these skills may cause your results to be less than what you want. Lacking them all causes no results at all.

Why does mental self talk work at all? It works because we were created with a subconscious mind. The subconscious mind is our internal, obedient servant. Like a good servant, it does whatever it is told to do—no more, no less. The subconscious mind does not think or reason, it just does whatever we program it to do.

If you allow it, other people can also program your subconscious mind. For example, if other people say, "You are a nerd," and you choose to believe that they are right, your subconscious mind accepts it as fact. Your subconscious mind then proceeds to alter your behavior so that you do indeed become a nerd. If, however, your attitude is, "That may be your opinion, but I know I am not a nerd," then your subconscious mind will not allow you to become a nerd.

The whole point of this side discussion is to tell you that you have the power to direct your subconscious mind by using your natural thought processes. Hence, you can achieve whatever you wish by deliberately programming your subconscious mind with clear, realistic, persistent directions.

Rarely is your subconscious mind impressed by one or two passing thoughts. Having a fleeting thought, "I want to be a millionaire," is highly unlikely to make any changes in your life. Your subconscious mind must be impressed, it must be taught, you must effectively let your obedient servant know exactly what you want. Usually, this involves repetition, consistency, and effective communication.

Repetition is pretty much self-explanatory. You repeatedly impress your desires on your subconscious through your thought processes, until you achieve what you want.

Consistency is a vital factor that most people trip themselves up on. For example, you want to change your career to become a paralegal and you program for that diligently for a couple weeks. Then you have second thoughts. You think it would be better to stay in your current job. A week later you decide what you really want is to sell life insurance. A couple weeks later you change your mind again, and so forth. You subconscious mind is confused. You keep giving it different directions. You have not given it clear, consistent instructions. It does the only thing it can do—NOTHING. If you consistently do this kind of programming, you, in effect, program your subconscious mind to not take you seriously at all. Then if you decide to program in earnest, your subconscious will ignore you—the "cry wolf" syndrome.

What about effective communication? This is where self talk, out loud, comes into play in a major way. When you talk out loud, you must first think (mental talk), and quite frequently you invoke mental visualization. Then you hear the words you are saying, which reenter your mind via auditory channels, and you reinforce your thoughts—sort of a double whammy. Two for the price of one.

In addition, talking out loud forces you to focus your concentration, which is vital to programming your subconscious. You know how easy it is for your mind to stray from thought to thought and wander aimlessly around when you are silently thinking. That is just the way minds tend to be. However, it is very difficult for your mind to wander when you are talking because it needs to stay focused in order for you to speak.

About fifteen years or so ago my daughter was in high school. One day I noticed her sitting in the living room. She would look at a book for a few minutes. Then she would look up from the book and stare into space. After about thirty minutes curiosity got the best of me and I asked what she was doing.

"I'm trying to memorize this darn poem that I have to recite in front of the class tomorrow," she replied.

"Are you going to give it silently in front of class?" I asked.

"Of course not."

"Then if you have to speak out loud, why not memorize it out loud?" I suggested.

She countered that people would think she was looney if she talked out loud to herself. When I pointed out that only her mother and I were present, she compromised by going into another room and shutting the door. I could hear her reading the poem out loud to herself. Within minutes she came out and announced, "I got it!"

The seeds for this book were probably planted due to that incident.

In the intervening years I have practiced self talk daily with great success.

It works! Now I offer it to you for your edification.

Formula For Success:
Mouth Power + Word Power = Personal Power

Chapter 3

Shape Up, Clown!

(How to Chew Yourself Out)

We all screw-up now and then. We do or say something we shouldn't have. Or we neglect to do or say something we should have. Most often these screw-ups are minor, although occasionally they are major.

Whether they are major or minor, you need to deal with them effectively when they occur, and then dismiss them from your conscious thought. There is no constructive value in dwelling on a screw-up.

It is okay, even advisable, to recall your screw-ups from time to time because it keeps you honest, so to speak, and helps you avoid repeating the mistakes. However, dwelling on screw-ups obsessively is counterproductive.

The reason you need to deal with it is so you can straighten out your programming. We screw-up for a variety of reasons: lack of concentration; we are tired; we act too hastily; we act without thinking things through first; we exercise faulty judgement, and so forth.

We need to give a loud, strong message to our obedient servant (our subconscious mind) that this is not the way we desire to be. We want to reduce our screw-ups to zero. This is called "chewing yourself out," and the most effective way to do it is out loud, in strong words, and with as much emotion as you can muster.

There are three elements to chewing yourself out:

1. Review the screw-up in detail—out loud.

2. Chastise yourself appropriately—out loud.

3. Tell yourself what corrective action you want—out loud.

With regard to item 2 above, you want to chastise yourself in a positive manner. Don't use words that are going to create more negative programming. For example, don't say something like, "Jones, you stupid idiot! You don't have the brains of a chicken egg!" Such words can be very detrimental.

Instead say something like,

"Jones, you sure used lousy judgment in this situation. You knew better. You are intelligent, but you got lax and allowed yourself to act like a jerk. You aren't a jerk, and I don't want you to act like one ever again! Do you hear me, Jones? I said never act like this again!"

Put emotion into your words. Shout at yourself. Really get with it. You are the coach, chewing out the team for a substandard performance.

There are an infinite number of "chewing out" scenarios, depending on the situation and on your personality. In a few moments I will provide several scenarios as guidelines, and you can take it from there.

When do you chew yourself out? As soon as practical after the screw-up. It may be immediately or it may be a day or so later. But do it as soon as you can while it is fresh in your mind. Too much delay will send a message to your obedient servant that you are tolerant of the screw-up, thus reinforcing unacceptable behavior.

Where do you do it? You definitely want to be alone when you chew yourself out. The reasons for this are obvious. For myself, I have three favorite places: In the bathtub; in the bathroom in front of the mirror; in the car while driving.

The bathtub is my favorite because there I am relaxed, alone, the door is shut, and I can think very clearly when I am up to my chin in warm, soothing water. I can talk vigorously out loud without disturbing my wife.

In front of a mirror is an excellent place for chewing yourself out. In fact, it is an excellent place for self talk for any purpose. You can look yourself straight in the eye and really take yourself to task. It is actually kind of fun, and it brings excellent results.

I use my car when I don't want to wait until I get home to take a bath to chew myself out. Usually, but not always, I use the car for a minor screw-up at work. For example, I make an error in writing a technical document that will cause me rework and embarrassment the next day. I can straighten myself out on this while driving home from work.

Here are three sample scenarios to give you some ideas on how to effectively use self talk (always out loud) to shape yourself up after a screw-up.

Scenario #1

You are driving to work and you are running a few minutes behind your usual schedule. A traffic light turns red just as you reach the intersection. You decide to proceed through anyway so you can make up some lost time (even though you could have easily stopped). A car sitting at the intersection makes a "jack rabbit" start the instant the driver gets the green light. You collide in the middle of the intersection. Results: No injuries; a couple thousand dollars damage to both cars. Cause: You screwed up by exercising poor judgment.

Later that day, in a quiet place where you are alone, you chew yourself out. Your dialog, which you *must* say 100% out loud and with as much emotion as you can muster, might go something like this:

Verbally review your screw-up

"I screwed up royally today! I caused an accident because I was in a hurry, and there wasn't even justification for being in a hurry.

"I was lucky this time. No one was injured, and insurance will take care of all but my two hundred dollar deductible payment."

Verbally chastise yourself

"I behaved in a totally irresponsible manner. That is not the way I want to be. That is not my usual behavior. I was not as clear-headed as I should have been, and there is no excuse for that. I am totally responsible for my actions, and I am ashamed of myself for letting myself down in this situation. I have no right to endanger the life of someone else, and yet that is exactly what I did. I acted in a completely unacceptable manner. (Here you really raise your voice at yourself). I SAID, I ACTED IN A COMPLETELY UNACCEPTABLE MANNER! NO EXCUSES!"

"I caused another person to be inconvenienced. I caused that person's property to be damaged. I HAVE NO RIGHT TO DO THAT! I AM ASHAMED OF MYSELF. I AM TRULY SORRY FOR MY THOUGHTLESS BEHAVIOR."

Verbally define what you are going to do

"I vow to myself to never do anything like that again. I SAID, I WILL NOT DO THAT AGAIN — EVER! I am a caring, responsible person by nature, but this time I screwed up. I don't want to ever screw-up again. I will strive to be even more alert, more caring, and more responsible in all my actions in the future.

I am now vowing to get all my priorities straight always. My first priority is to never endanger another person's life or property. There is no rational excuse for endangering another person's life or property, and I shall not behave in such an irresponsible manner again.

I forgive myself for this thoughtless behavior, but I shall never forget it because by remembering, I shall strengthen my resolve to do better and to not repeat the behavior."

This scenario is a sample to give you one idea of how to chew yourself out when you screw-up in a serious situation. Within this concept you can develop your own approach and use words with which you are comfortable.

If you use a mirror for this self talk session, you might want to address your image in the mirror by name instead of saying "I." Such as "Jones, you really screwed up royally today!" And so forth.

By actually performing a self talk session such as this, you program your subconscious mind (your obedient servant) to:

1. Acknowledge your behavior truthfully.

2. Cleanse yourself of negative programming.

3. Institute and reinforce new positive programming to guide your future behavior.

You have given your obedient servant clear instructions concerning what you want and do not want in your future behavior.

Most of us like to be a clown once in a while. When done in good taste and with sensitivity, clowning is fun and pleasant.

But what about those times when the clowning is in poor taste and is insensitive? An innocent person gets embarrassed and hurt. When you are the clown who caused the hurt, how do you handle it? In scenario #2, I address such a situation. I have arbitrarily chosen a male clown and a female victim of the clowning. The scenario is valid, however, regardless of who does what to whom.

Scenario #2

A co-worker is escorting a new employee around the department to introduce her. The new employee has a full figure that strains the snug, but very pretty, dress she is wearing.

When she is introduced to you, you say, "Glad to meet you. Welcome to the department. In case no one warned you, I am the department clown."

She smiles and says, "Every department has a clown. Glad to meet you."

"You are wearing a very pretty dress," you add. "Too bad they didn't have it in your size."

Then you grin like you had just said the funniest line ever written, only no one else is smiling. The new employee is fighting back tears. The co-worker quickly rushes her away and tries changing the subject in an attempt to mollify the situation.

You stand there alone. Your grin disappears as you realize you have acted like the west end of an east-bound horse.

What do you do now?

You cannot undo what you said. But even the west end of an east-bound horse has enough sense to know that the situation must be made right.

First: Head directly to the men's room and sit on one of the thrones, which is apropos considering what you did. Tell yourself out loud that you behaved like the west end of an east-bound horse (in more graphic terms) and you are sorry.

Second: Still using self talk say,

"(The woman's name), this is (your name). I am sorry for my crude, insensitive remark. I know I hurt you, and I have no right to do that. I thought I was being funny, but I wasn't. Sometimes clowns get carried away. I didn't intend to hurt you. I am truly sorry. Please forgive me."

Third: Go to a telephone and call a florist. Order a beautiful floral arrangement to be sent as quickly as possible today to the offended woman at her work station. Dictate a sincere note of apology to accompany the flowers. Try to arrange the delivery within the hour if you can—even if you have to pay extra. Even if the flowers cost $40 and you only earn $4 an hour—you do this. This is an absolute step. Self talk by itself does not get you off the hook in all situations. Here is a case where you must augment your self talk with concrete action.

Fourth: Shortly after the flowers are delivered, you go in person to apologize. You invite her to lunch—your treat—for that day or the next day. You offended her deeply without justification and you must make amends. If she declines your lunch invitation, don't press the issue. The matter is closed.

Fifth: That evening make some time to use self talk to chew yourself out using scenario #1 as a model. Be sure to apologize to the woman again. Forgive yourself. Resolve to grow up and discontinue being the department clown. All this must be done using self talk, always out loud. Repeat this self talk session for two more nights, then you can forget it. Scenario #2 illustrates that there are times when self talk alone is not sufficient because of the seriousness of what you have done.

In scenario #1 you would also have had to make financial restitution if your insurance had not covered it. As it is (with scenario #1) you had to pay your deductible, pay a traffic citation, probably had to appear in traffic court and pay court costs, and probably had your insurance rates increased.

Screw-ups are usually expensive. That is one of the reasons self talk is so important. Self talk enables you to program yourself to eliminate or greatly reduce your screw-ups.

Before we leave scenario #2, I want to call your attention to something else that is different. In addition to apologizing to the woman face to face, I also twice directed the clown to apologize to the woman using self talk when the clown was alone.

There are two reasons for this. First, there is an excellent chance that the woman will receive the message subliminally. Second, the clown needs to condition his subconscious to be more caring and sensitive.

Talking out loud to someone who is not physically present is a powerful mechanism for communicating subliminally with that person as well as for communicating with your obedient servant (your subconscious mind). Get in the habit of doing this. In subsequent chapters I will show you how to do this for other kinds of situations.

In scenario #3 we have a situation where self talk alone would completely atone for a screw-up. Scenario #3 is an actual situation that happened to me in the early 1960s on a subway train in New York City. The people who did it to me did not use self talk or any other sort of restitution. I will hypothe-size what they should have done using self talk.

Scenario #3

I was an out-of-towner in New York on business. My hotel was in uptown Manhattan and my busi-ness appointment was across town in downtown Manhattan. I decided to take the subway because it is the fastest and least expensive way to get around in New York City.

When I boarded the subway train, the car was only about half full. I picked out a seat and settled in. After a couple more train stops the car was completely jammed with people. All the seats were filled and peo-ple were standing in every available space, hanging onto straps or poles.

A woman, who was visibly quite pregnant and carrying a parcel, boarded the car and stood, hang-ing onto a strap about a half-car away from where I was sitting. None of the men seated near her offered her a seat.

Being born and raised a midwesterner, where customs and manners are more traditional, I couldn't tolerate letting a pregnant woman stand while I sat. I stood up, caught her eye and said, "M'am, you can have this seat."

I'll never forget the two things that happened next. She glared at me, then sneered and said in a voice as cold and as hard as tempered steel, "What are you, some kind of freak!" Then she turned her back to me, continuing to stand there holding onto the strap.

Simultaneously, a scruffy young man who, along with several equally scruffy friends, had been standing near me forced himself between me (I was still half standing at that point) and my seat and claimed it for his own. His tough friends roared with laughter. They thought it was all very funny.

My first instinct was to have a confrontation with the scruffy young man, but better sense prevailed. I could have ended up with a knife in my belly, so I rode on to my stop in silence, burning with anger over the extreme rudeness of the woman and the young man.

I related the incident to the president of the company with whom I had my business appointment. He was a native New Yorker who had grown up in the streets of Brooklyn.

"That is just the way it is here, he said. "You mid-westerners are naive."

What had been anger now turned to pity for these people who had allowed themselves to become so calloused and insensitive. I instantly harbored no bad feelings toward them. They had created a hell for themselves that I had no intention of adding to with bad feelings.

In those days self talk didn't exist yet. And even if it had, that woman and young man would probably not have had the sensitivity to use it.

Let's hypothesize what self talk they might have used. They couldn't have sent me a note saying they were sorry for their conduct because they didn't know my name or where I lived. But they could have chastised themselves for their behavior, they could have said "Sorry about that," and they could have resolved to change their behavior. They could have done this using self talk, and it would have made a difference for the better, but they probably didn't.

Could have, but didn't. Maybe that is the difference between unacceptable behavior and acceptable behavior.

The people who could have but didn't are the ones who degenerate into calloused, crude people with unacceptable behavior.

The people who could have and do are the ones who lift themselves to new heights of refinement and have acceptable behavior.

One practice that can make the difference between unacceptable and acceptable is SELF TALK.

Think about it.

Formula For Success:
Mouth Power + Word Power = Personal Power

Chapter 4

Hello, God, I Need Some Help

(How to Pray More Effectively)

First of all, this is not a chapter on religion. I respect everyone's religious convictions and their right to follow their convictions. What I say in this chapter is not intended to impinge on personal religious matters in any way.

I do not personally belong to any religious sect. However, I am spiritual. I do believe in the existence of one supreme being, and I do believe that it is possible to conduct successful two-way communication with that supreme being. The two-way communication with that supreme being is called prayer.

In this chapter I am going to discuss self talk and a different perspective on prayer than perhaps you have thought about before. You may want to

31

integrate what I talk about into the framework of your own beliefs and practices in order to have more effective two-way communication with God.

How many times have you heard someone say, "My prayers were never answered," or a similar sort of statement? I've heard it hundreds of times.

I will tell you right now: "There is no such thing as an unanswered prayer!"

All true prayers are always answered—100% of the time—absolutely—no exceptions.

What appears to be an unanswered prayer is really one of the following:

1. You really didn't give an effective prayer in the first place, or

2. You didn't listen for or recognize the answer, or

3. You got an answer but it wasn't the one you wanted so you considered the prayer to be unanswered.

In this chapter, I will discuss only item #1 above because I believe the major problem with praying is that most people do not know how to pray effectively. I will discuss a way to increase the effectiveness of your prayers.

Items #2 and #3 above require a significant change in your mental attunement, which is dealt with in great detail in my book, *Beyond Hypnosis*, in case you are interested in pursuing the matter further.

From the time I was a little tyke until my late thirties, I was a member of six different religious sects. With variations, most Sunday sermons went something like this:

The clergyman would offer a prayer/sermon that lasted from thirty minutes to an hour and a half. He would pace up and down, shouting, sometimes weeping, and always waving his arms dramatically. He would ask God to do everything, from saving us from the grasshopper scourge that was destroying our crops, to ensuring every congregation member a happy, successful life. His oratory was profound and second only to Daniel Webster at his best. It was quite a show. Everyone was emotionally moved. (Today's televangelists are a current example of what I am talking about). Afterwards, we all felt we had prayed properly, and we went on our merry way until we could have another good prayer session next Sunday.

Know what? We never were saved from the grasshopper scourge, and a large percentage of the congregation never did have happy or successful lives.

Did God let us down? Of course not. We let ourselves down. We had not prayed at all. We had deluded ourselves. All we had really done was watch a drama, and all the clergyman had done was perform. To call it prayer is ludicrous.

"But we were on our knees. Our heads were bowed. Doesn't that count as prayer?"

No, it doesn't count. Kneeling and bowing are human physical actions to pay respect to, or to show subservience to, another human being or to impress other people that you are a reverent person.

To impress God, you must bow your heart.

"But I was attentive at the prayer meeting. I listened to every word. Doesn't that count?"

No, it doesn't count. Prayer is a personal action that you must take to open up your communication path to God. Listening to someone else conduct an oratory doesn't qualify at all.

You must bow your heart, use your own mind, your own words, and your own mouth. Then you have it!

How? When? Is it difficult?

No, it is not difficult. It is the easiest, most natural thing in the world to do. Now I will show you how and when, and will give you some examples.

How to give an effective prayer

Talk out loud. There are times when it is prudent to pray silently, and I'll discuss this shortly. But 99% of the time, talk to God out loud.

No, God isn't hard of hearing. Talking out loud is for your benefit, not God's. By praying out loud, you must first think the words and then say them. Then you hear yourself saying them, which reinforces the prayer in your mind and heart. Talking also forces you to focus your awareness, which intensifies the effectiveness of your prayer.

When you pray mentally, your mind is prone to quickly stray onto other thoughts because that is just the way minds prefer to operate. It takes a very disciplined mind to concentrate intensely enough on silent prayer to be effective.

On the other hand, it is very difficult for the mind to slip away when you are actively talking because the mind's attention is required in order to talk. That is just the way it is.

So use self talk. Pray out loud.

One exception. It is prudent to pray silently if you are praying when other people are around. There are several reasons for this.

First, what you are praying about is no one's business.

Second, if you pray out loud around others who are not also praying, they will feel uncomfortable. The purpose of prayer is to communicate with God, not to make others feel uncomfortable.

Third, can you imagine walking through Macy's department store while bursting forth in prayer? There is a reasonable likelihood that the security people would quickly escort you out; they would not likely be understanding.

The rule of thumb is to use common sense. "I will feel foolish praying out loud," you protest.

"Why?" I ask. "You sing out loud, don't you? There is no difference between singing and speaking, except that singing is speaking in a melodious way."

Society, in its infinite ignorance, has conditioned you to believe that you aren't supposed to talk out loud when you are alone. Rubbish! Society is grossly in error on this.

Stop letting society dictate to you on such an important and personal matter as prayer.

God is the only one you need to be concerned about, and He wants to hear from you.

So talk! Out loud! It works!

When to pray

I do 90% of my praying while alone in my car driving. I always speak out loud. No radio playing. Both hands on the wheel. I talk as though I had my best friend riding along with me, which of course is exactly who I do have with me in the car.

Isn't this hazardous? No, it isn't. Anyone who is unable to drive and talk at the same time ought not to be driving. However, if this is a big concern to you, pick another place for your praying.

For example, you might pray in your home, in another room away from the rest of your family, or while you are in the yard, pulling weeds. The opportunities are extensive.

I pray out loud in my office at work sometimes. I do keep my voice down because there are people in adjacent offices and in the hallway.

If you are serious about improving the effectiveness of your prayers, you will creatively seek out places in which to do it.

What to say

Talk conversationally, just as you would with your best friend. Say what is on your mind. Ask questions. Seek whatever help you need. You don't need elaborate oratory—in fact oratory is probably a detriment. Keep it simple and straight from the heart.

The most powerful prayer I have ever uttered was one word. A man was dying and was depending on me to help him. I didn't know what to do. I rolled my eyes upward, bowed my heart, and silently screamed, "Help!" I got the response immediately in a powerful, profound way. The story of this incident is detailed in my book, *Beyond Hypnosis*. The result was that I was able to help the man, and he lived another five years. The way I helped him was something I could never have dreamed up myself. I got the solution from God immediately in response to my one word prayer, "Help!"

I mentioned that I rolled my eyes upwards. Get in the habit of doing this occasionally during prayer or if you want to remember something. When you roll your eyes upward, you trigger alpha brain activity, which is the area where the most powerful prayer can take place. A detailed technical explanation of this phenomenon can be found in my first book, *Hypnosis*, if you are interested.

If you are out of work and need a job to support your family, say out loud something like: "Father, I need help. Please guide me to find a job so I can take proper care of my family. Thank you." That's all. Keep it simple and straightforward. I think you get the idea.

The content of your prayers is entirely your business. I do, however, offer one thing to think about. Don't drag out a laundry list of things you want God to do for you. When He created you He gave you a great deal of ability to do for yourself and He expects you to use that ability. Don't sit on your duff expecting a handout. Do the best you can, and His help will always be available.

Earlier I mentioned that you should "bow your heart" as part of praying effectively. This comes for free when you pray out loud. The humbling, focused experience of talking out loud to God automatically causes you to bow your heart.

Start talking. You'll see.

Formula For Success:
Mouth Power + Word Power = Personal Power

Chapter 5

Listen Up,
You So and So

(How to Use Self Talk on Your Boss)

Now, because of the very sensitive nature of the material in this chapter, my publisher asked me to remind the reader that Self Talk is only spoken out loud to yourself, where you cannot be heard by other people. In the particular instance of this chapter, I want to reinforce that point. Do not say these words out loud, or even "under your breath" to your employer! *We don't want to get you fired! In addition, I want to point out that we can use words in self talk that we would perhaps never speak out loud to other people. The words we employ in self talk work better when they invoke strong emotions. It's the emotion you feel when using self talk that is the source of power for bringing about the results you want.*

Most of us at sometime or other work under the supervision of someone else. We have a boss. The boss is either a Sweet Old Buddy or a Sweet Old Babe (S.O.B. for short).

Frequently the two-way communication between us and the boss leaves a lot to be desired. The boss doesn't let us know what he/she expects of us—or changes his/her mind—or doesn't communicate at all—or plays favorites, and so forth.

Often we are intimidated by the boss to the extent that we get either tongue-tied or at a loss for words when we have the opportunity to speak to him/her. Sometimes we are thwarted in our attempts to talk to the boss—he/she doesn't have time or gets interrupted by a phone call or by someone regarded as being more important than us.

Sound familiar?

We don't have any trouble thinking of the things we want to say to the boss, do we? In our minds we speak eloquently, with confidence and firmness. Somehow, however, we never seem to get around to actually saying those things to the boss. As a result, we don't seem to get the raises we think we deserve. We get passed over for promotion. The exciting job assignments are given to someone else. When favors are handed out, our name is not on the list. We feel that we don't even exist as far as the boss is concerned.

In all fairness, the problem is not always the boss. Sometimes we are the problem, or at least part of the problem.

In this chapter, however, it doesn't matter where the problem lies. This chapter is concerned only with improving your communications with your boss, and you will do it in an off-beat way.

Bosses are supposed to be pro-active. It is incumbent on them to establish and maintain effective communication with their people. That responsibility goes with the job. Therefore, this chapter is devoted to getting your boss to take the initiative to improve communications with you. Of course, you have to do your part, too, but in a more passive way.

First of all, making this happen does not involve you talking face to face with the boss. Instead you will talk out loud, using self talk, when there is no one at all with you.

You are going to tell the boss everything you want, in any language you want, with whatever emotion you want. You can ask questions. There are no restrictions on what you say or how you say it, and no one will hear it except you.

Sounds weird, doesn't it?

Though it sounds weird, there is in fact solid rationale in doing this. It works, and here is why:

1. Humans communicate with each other in several different ways: Verbally; body language; and subliminally. Subliminally is where self talk comes in, and we will discuss this further in a few moments.

2. Venting your mind out loud has a cathartic effect on your mind and your emotions.

You purge yourself of pent-up frustrations. Your mind starts functioning more clearly. You begin to see your communication problem more accurately. Your role in the whole situation becomes more evident. This is a valuable, necessary self-healing, self-balancing process.

3. Talking out loud forces you to focus intently on your relationship with your boss. In so doing, you plant the seeds for greater understanding of yourself and of your boss. Successful communication has its roots in "understanding."

Let's talk a little more about the subliminal communication referred to in item #1 above. Subliminal means "below the level of conscious awareness." In other words, we also communicate at a mental energy level without being consciously aware of it. This may well be the most powerful of all communication, yet few people even think about it or deliberately try to use it effectively. Mental telepathy, for example, is one form of subliminal communication.

Self talk activates subliminal communication. What you say out loud to your boss causes you to transmit the message to him/her, even though the boss is not physically present.

The boss will receive the message without being aware of it. The stronger and more persistent you send the message, the stronger it is impressed on the boss' mind.

So with self talk to your boss, three beneficial things start occurring simultaneously:

1. Your message gets to the boss subliminally.

2. You clear your mind for better perception.

3. You gain better understanding of the situation.

As a result, you begin to change a little, your boss begins to change a little, things begin to happen to promote a better rapport between you and your boss. Before you know it, you and your boss have gained a mutual respect and understanding. More favorable things begin to happen to you.

More often than not, the change begins in a subtle, innocuous way.

For example, using self talk you have told your boss repeatedly for about a month that you would like to have a better job in the company. One day you both "coincidentally" arrive at the water cooler for a drink of water at the same time, and the water jug is empty. There are no full replacement jugs on hand.

The boss remarks, "Damn. I'm so thirsty I could spit cotton balls."

"I'll arrange to get some water jugs if you'd like," you say, perhaps a little timidly because you aren't quite certain how to do it.

"Great. I'd appreciate it. Ron in Purchasing usually takes care of this, but we've had him swamped with other work."

"No problem."

"Let me know when you get it."

You go to Ron in Purchasing and ask him what to do. You proceed to do it, and the delivery man brings you two bottles that afternoon.

A few days later Ron is so swamped with work that he asks the boss for help and mentions your name because he was impressed with your initiative.

The boss promotes you to assistant buyer to help Ron. You are on your way up. You have caught the boss's eye in a favorable way. It is only a matter of time before you become a buyer, then a senior buyer, and so on.

In reality, the response to your self talk to the boss will most often materialize just as simply and as quickly as I've just described. Sometimes it takes longer or becomes more involved, but if you persist with your self talk you will get results.

Let's talk about results a bit. Your self talk should be directly geared to the results you desire. For example, if you want a salary increase, don't say something like, "Boss, you blind, stupid jerk, I want more money. You are a tightwad and a skinflint. Loosen up, Scrooge!"

That speech will net you zero! Remember you are subliminally sending a message to your boss. You are calling him/her unflattering names such as "stupid," "jerk," "Scrooge," "tightwad," etc. In addition, you are not giving any reasons why you deserve a salary increase. No boss would give you a dime under those circumstances.

That speech would have quite an adverse effect. The boss would begin to dislike you more and more without consciously knowing why. You would have undercut your position permanently, insofar as having a future working for this specific boss.

Let's look at three sample scenarios for self talk to your boss for different situations. First we'll start with asking for a salary increase, since we are already on that subject.

In these scenarios, where I use the word "boss," substitute your boss's name (Mr. Smith, Ms. Jones).

Scenario #1

Your need for a salary increase:

"Boss, this is (your name) in the Records Department. I've worked here over a year now and have not had a salary increase. I work hard, and my work is good. When you hired me, you admitted the records were in a shambles. I've fixed it all up now. Our records are up to date and I've instituted beneficial changes. You never come into my department to even see what I am doing. I know my job isn't as visible and glamorous as sales or advertising, but my job is important. Please start coming in to the Records Department to see what I have done and am doing. Ask me questions. I need some "warm fuzzies" too, just like other people. I know you are busy, but I should be on your list of necessary things to do just like other people. And I do need, and do deserve, a salary increase. My expenses are no different than any one else's. I believe you strive to be a fair person, but in my case I think I have slipped your mind because my job is out of your immediate sight. Boss, please put (your name) on your list for a salary increase and for more professional attention at work. Thank you."

The script for scenario #1 is structured very powerfully, and it will get results. The tone of the dialog is positive. You don't call the boss nasty names. You present your case factually, and you give the boss the benefit of any doubt even though the boss may not deserve it. Your approach is professional. These are features of self talk that you need to consider for any scenario you devise.

For scenario #1, I recommend you pick a self talk time that does not coincide with your boss's working hours. At work your boss' mind is going a mile a minute with job-related problems, and his mind may not become as impregnated with your self talk message as it might at a more peaceful time.

Try for off-work hours, or even when you think he might be sleeping. Try during prime television hours also. Two times that a person's mind is especially susceptible to subliminal impressions are during sleep and while watching television.

Scenario #2

Your boss has one major failing. He thrives on ethnic and sexist remarks and jokes. Any offensive joke, whether it be sexual, racist, Jewish, Polish, Italian, sick, Irish and so forth, is in his repertoire. He never misses an opportunity to pollute someone's ears with his verbal garbage.

People have walked away from him when he starts his spiel, but he doesn't get the message. Several have told him outright they aren't interested in hearing his jokes, but he persists anyway. He has the skin of a rhinoceros and the sensitivity of a barnyard goat.

How do you handle this with self talk? The first thing to do is to forget about being a nice person. This slob does not deserve easy treatment. In fact, he is not likely to even respond to anything other than 'barroom' language.

You have to talk in language he can comprehend. You don't need to stoop to gutter language (unless you choose to), but you do need to be harsh, direct, and tough. Next to mentally unstable people, these crude, offensive, insensitive boors are the most difficult people to reach through self talk or any other method.

In my own experience, I find that self talk is more effective on this type person than other kinds of communication. Also in my experience, I find a lower success rate with these crude people than with any other kind of person I've dealt with. There is one exception—mentally ill or mentally unstable persons do not seem to respond well at all to self talk. I am not an authority on mental illness, so I have no explanation for this. It is just an observation from my limited experience in trying to reach mentally unstable people through self talk.

Now back to this crude boss. How do you handle him with self talk? Here is one suggested approach. Using it as a model, you can devise your own for your own situation.

"Boss, you are a crude, disgusting jerk! I cannot stand your filthy, rotten jokes and remarks. Nobody can stand you because of your garbage mouth. Is that filthy mouth the same one you eat with? Nobody has any respect for you.

"I am going to give you until (state a specific date) to show some sign of positive change in your behavior. If you have not stopped your rotten, unwelcome remarks by (say the date again) I am going to report you to (state specifically to whom, upper management, the civil rights commission, the personnel director, etc.). Do you hear me, garbage mouth (state the S.O.B.'s name)? I said I am going to report you to (state to whom again) if you don't stop telling offensive jokes and making offensive statements by (repeat the date)."

Then make your word good. If there is no improvement in the time period, make your formal complaint just as you promised. To be fair—not that this jerk deserves fair—wait at least a month for improvement to show. Remember, these clods are very difficult to get through to.

If there is one particular kind of offensive talk the boss is guilty of, hammer on it in your self talk. Most often, it is probably sexual. If sexual, you might even want to include a statement like: "Your sexual remarks make me want to vomit. You personally have the sexual appeal of vomit (or some other appropriate word)."

Show this jerk no mercy. He/she must change or be replaced. This kind of behavior has no place in our society, and especially in our workplace. There is absolutely no excuse for anyone in a supervisory position acting like this. It does not have to be tolerated.

Scenario #1 shows how to deal with your boss in a typical work situation. Scenario #2 shows how to deal with a boss (or anyone else for that matter) who has the social graces of a wart hog. In scenario #3 we will deal with an often overlooked aspect of employee-management relationships.

Scenario #3

Most bosses are good people and are good bosses. They, just like you, do their very best every day. They strive to be fair and to provide the best leadership they can. Rarely does anyone tell them "Thank you" or "You are doing a good job." Bosses need to get "warm fuzzies" once in a while just like everyone else.

One problem is, how do you give your boss warm fuzzies without appearing to try to "kiss-up" the boss? Even sincere remarks can appear to your co-workers and to the boss as being "kiss-up" attempts. You don't want that. So what do you do?

If you guessed self talk, you guessed correctly.

I strongly urge the frequent use of self talk to give warm fuzzies to good bosses and to other people, too. It is good for them, and it is good for you. Giving warm fuzzies helps you retain your membership in the human race as opposed to being a card carrying jerk in the disguise of being a human.

A warm fuzzy self talk session might go something like this:

"Boss, this is (your name). I think you are doing a good job and I just want to say thank you."

If the boss had done something in particular that you wanted to tell him about, then do it. For example, the boss may have had the courage to promote a minority person into a supervisory job, and you knew he had to do battle with upper management in order to make it happen. This certainly would be an excellent occasion to use self talk for praising your boss. In this case, you might also want to use self talk to praise your boss to his/her boss.

What it amounts to is that via self talk you can reach any person in your company with whatever message you wish. A powerful tool, is it not?

Here are a few other work situations you may want to use self talk on:

1. The boss is a slave driver. Tell him/her to back off, using a scenario #1 variation that you can devise.

2. The boss has no backbone—doesn't back his/her people up.

3. The boss has a hygiene problem. Or more often, a co-worker has the hygiene problem and you want to tell the boss to do something about it.

4. The boss doesn't delegate authority, yet is never available for consultation (always in meetings, on trips, etc.).

Using self talk, you can redo your entire work situation. If you get some co-workers to also use self talk for the same situation, you can collectively bring about dramatic change in a hurry. The power of collective mouths (self talk) is awesome!

Formula For Success:
Mouth Power + Word Power = Personal Power

Chapter 6

Fraidy Cat!

(Using Self Talk to Control Fear)

In the spring of 1982 my wife and I took a seventy-three day trip through the southern and southeastern United States in our motor home. One evening at sundown we pulled in for the night at a state campground near Waurika, Oklahoma. It was a beautiful campground, and ours was the only camper there.

"I wonder why no one else is here?" my wife asked as she tuned in a local radio station on our portable radio.

As if on cue, the announcer gave his station's call letters and said, "Welcome to Waurika, Oklahoma, the rattlesnake capital of the world; where there are more rattlesnakes per square mile than anywhere else in the world."

My blood ran cold. I was too tired from driving to push on further. We both needed rest. But I wasn't about to go outside. Fortunately, our motor home is 100% self-contained so there was no need to have to go outside, and we didn't.

There may not have been a snake of any kind within a mile, but I wasn't about to find out. The radio announcer's greeting was enough to trigger the only fear I have ever had—a fear of snakes. So I remained captive in my motor home by a fear that may not have even had any real basis.

Frankly, I was a little ashamed of myself. Fear is powerful, and it can dominate you.

In those days I had been using self talk sporadically for a limited number of purposes such as memory improvement, affirmations for success, job interview preparation, etc. I had not yet discovered the enormous power of self talk for virtually any situation.

It never occurred to me at that moment to use self talk to control my fear. So I remained captive by my fear. I never forgot the feeling of helplessness I had. Intellectually, I knew I was not behaving rationally, but fear is a powerful emotion and it overpowered my rational reasoning.

Fear is a terrible thing to have. It is crippling. In the ensuing years, I developed my expertise in self talk over a wide range of uses. But I had not yet done any work on fear control through self talk. There was no need. I had never had another potential encounter with a snake, and I had no fears other than concerning snakes.

Then one day we planned a week's camping trip into the Rocky Mountains of Colorado.

Snakes! The mental imagery jumped into my mind, and my blood ran cold. The mountains, I knew, are a haven for all sorts of snakes. They are a haven for all sorts of wild life, but only the snakes concerned me.

If I were to meet a bear face to face it would not invoke terror in me. I'd be concerned, of course, and would get quickly out of its way, but I would remain in control. But mention snakes, and all control would go out the window.

This I knew had to change, and I was determined to make it change now. My thoughts this time immediately turned to self talk because I had seen first-hand what a powerful force self talk was in a vast array of circumstances.

The night before we were to leave on our Rocky Mountain camping trip I settled into my warm bath water and had a serious self talk session concerning my fear of snakes. As I recall, it went something like this:

"Hewitt, you are intelligent and reasonable. You are a logical thinker. So why do you think so illogically when it comes to snakes?"

"I don't know."

"Has a snake ever hurt you?"

"No."

"You know that snakes play an important role in the balance of nature, don't you?"

"Yes, I know that."

"You can walk faster than a snake can slither, so one cannot catch you. You have the power to kill them easily. You can outsmart them.

"In fact, snakes can't do much at all except hang around and eat bugs and rodents. They are doing you a favor. They are your friends because they control pests.

"They don't even like to be around people and avoid people whenever possible. If you don't like being around them, stay off their turf."

I continued on in that vein for a while. Then I told myself that the next time I encountered a snake, I would not be afraid, I would be calm and in control, and would react no differently than if I had encountered any other creature. I reinforced these self talk commands, out loud of course, several more times. My total bathtub self talk session probably lasted no more than 30 minutes.

We had set up camp just a couple of hours when I encountered a snake.

I was standing, legs wide apart, drinking in the majesty of the mountains, the freshness of the pine trees, and the rush of the white water river next to our campsite. I glanced down and there was a two-foot gopher snake slithering between my legs like it was passing under the Arch de Triumph enroute to someplace important.

There was no fear on my part. I saw the snake as just another creature doing the best it could to get along in the world.

Nearby was a small, fallen branch from a tree. It was about the thickness of my little finger and perhaps three feet long. I stepped over and picked up the branch.

I carefully slid the branch under the snake's belly about midpoint so as not to hurt or frighten it. I picked it up on the stick gently and even spoke out loud to it, "I am going to move you to a safer place, little buddy. You could get injured if you stay here."

I walked about 100 feet away, across a dirt road, and onto the slope of a grassy hill where I gently lowered it into the grass. It quickly slithered away. Again I spoke out loud, "I'll make you a deal. You stay here, and I'll stay over there at my campsite."

The fear was gone. I felt good about myself. I handled the situation calmly and appropriately. I didn't harm the snake, and it posed to harm to me. At no time was I even a little bit anxious or nervous. I saw the snake in an entirely different light than ever before.

There is no doubt whatsoever in my mind but that my self talk in the bathtub was responsible for my overcoming the fear. My self talk with the snake was an extension of my bathtub session—a concluding speech in a manner of speaking.

I view my encounter with the snake so soon after my self talk session as being a test to show me that self talk works.

Since then I have not had an encounter with a snake and probably never will. Fear is like that. Once you face it and conquer it, it is gone forever and there is no need for further testing.

I strongly recommend to you: If you have a fear, use self talk to understand the fear and to get rid of the fear.

Not all fears may disappear as quickly and easily as mine did. Some fears may require extensive self talk sessions over a period of time. Some fears may be so deeply ingrained that professional therapy may be required, but self talk can still help by making the therapy more effective.

Fear imprisons people. Self talk frees people.

Become free—start using self talk today and every day.

Formula For Success:
Mouth Power + Word Power = Personal Power

Chapter 7

Psst! Have I Got a Deal for You!

(Using Self Talk to Purchase a Car)

Purchasing a motor vehicle is one of the most precarious experiences most of us ever undertake. The odds are stacked heavily in favor of the car dealer, and when you walk into his showroom you have about as much chance as when you drop a silver dollar into a slot machine in Las Vegas.

Think about it. You purchase a car perhaps once every four years or so. The car salesman sells cars every day. Which of you has the most experience in the car business, you or the car salesman? The car salesman of course. So your chances of getting skinned are pretty good.

In all fairness, most new car dealers have cleaned up their act in recent years and strive to be reputable—but they are in business to make as much money as they can, and you are their money source. In my experience I find that used car dealers tend to have less integrity than new car dealers. In any case, it is still a "buyer beware" market and the best you can do is to minimize how much you get skinned.

You need all the help you can get when buying a car. Self talk can be a significant help. I'll show you how.

I had not used self talk for purchasing an automobile until June 1990, even though I had been using it for years for other purposes. It hadn't even occurred to me that self talk could be used for buying a car. It took two previous experiences with car dealers to crystallize the idea in my mind for using self talk to buy a car.

Let me tell you about those two previous experiences first so you can see how I finally evolved my self talk approach to buying a car.

In early 1985 I thought it might be a good idea to buy my wife a new car and let her old one, a 1972 model, be a back-up car. There was a car she liked, so we went into the dealership nearest our home.

The salesman quickly wrote out some figures on a piece of paper and we began dickering. Within minutes he decreased his asking price until our payments would be $250 a month for forty-eight months with a $1000 down payment. An excellent deal on a new convertible, fully loaded with extras, that carried a sticker price of $15,000. He never even argued with us. It was the easiest deal we had ever made.

He said, "I'll take this paper back to the typist to be written into a formal contract. It should be ready in about fifteen minutes." Then he disappeared with the paper.

Something kept gnawing at my mind, but I didn't know what the problem was. So I verbalized my thoughts, ostensibly to my wife, although in retrospect I now realize I was really talking to myself.

"Something isn't quite right," I said. "What do I need to know? What questions do I need to ask? What am I overlooking?"

Immediately I got a mental message: "Read the contract very carefully before signing it."

Just a split second after I got the mental message, my wife said to me, "You had better check the contract carefully. I don't feel right about this either."

The salesman reappeared, typed contract in hand, and a cheshire grin plastered on his face. He had the contract folded to the last page (the signature page).

"Just sign here, and you can drive your new convertible away within minutes," he said, tapping his finger by the signature line while thrusting a ballpoint pen at me with his other hand.

"I am going to read it first," I said.

"No need to," he said. "It is exactly as we agreed on. I'll tell you what it says to save you time."

He picked up the contract, flipped quickly to the first page, and pointed to two entries as he spoke. "See, two-fifty a month and a thousand down just as we discussed." He quickly flipped back to the signature page. "The rest is just the standard mumbo jumbo about warranties and responsibilities."

I laid the pen aside and picked up the contract. "I'll read it first," I said.

The cheshire grin disappeared. He walked off mumbling that he would be back when I finished.

Within a few seconds I discovered the problem. He had put in sixty months instead of forty-eight as the term of the loan. That would increase my cost by $3000. No wonder he didn't argue about the deal. He had planned on rooking me in the contract.

When he returned, I confronted him. He said sixty months was what we had agreed on. I asked him to get the paper he had written originally. He said he had thrown it away.

"How difficult is it for you to get it from the waste basket?" I asked sarcastically because I was now certain in my mind that the sixty months was not an inadvertent typographical mistake.

He made a face expressing displeasure. "I'll see if I can find it."

When he didn't return within five minutes, my wife and I got up and walked out. He must have been watching because he came running after us.

"The waste basket was emptied into the dumpster already, but if you come back in I am sure we can work out a deal."

"Don't insult our intelligence," I snapped. "You lied, and you tried to cheat us. We shall never return to this dealership."

We drove away. My wife was so angered that she said she didn't want a car for a while. Although I didn't recognize it at the time, the seeds for self talk in buying a car had been sown in my mind.

It was nearly two more years before we tried again. This second experience watered the seeds and started them growing.

It was November, 1986. The 1987 models were out. I noticed my wife had been looking at new car ads in the magazines, so I suggested that she might want to shop for one.

"I know what I want," she said. "A Chrysler New Yorker, because it has class without being a snob about it."

"Then we will go out this coming Saturday to look."

Let me digress a moment to tell you something about my wife because it is germane to the story. She is second to none when it comes to bartering. She is the personification of the art of bartering.

Each day for the five days until Saturday, she told and re-told me her plan in detail. It went something like this:

- I am going to lay down the ground rules with the salesman immediately. If he doesn't play by my rules, I walk out and I will not return, no matter what.

- Colors that are totally unacceptable to me are black, burgundy, green, and white.

- I will not accept the "emergency" spare tire. It must be a full-size spare that exactly matches the ones on the car and there must be no extra charge for it.

- I want the top of the line AM-FM stereo radio and cassette player.

- I must have automatic, air conditioning, turbo, wire wheel covers . . . she went on to list every option she wanted.

- I will take my checkbook, and will write out a check for a 100% cash deal. No financing.

- I will not dicker. The salesman will have one chance to quote me his best price. If it is higher than I am willing to pay, I will walk out and not buy.

- I will not tolerate the salesman showing me any car other than one that meets the specifications I have told him.

- I will not tolerate the salesman having to run back and forth to the sales manager to shave a few dollars off the price.

- The price the salesman quotes me must be one total price that includes all taxes, dealer add-ons, and so forth. If he tries to add any amount onto the quoted price after we make the deal, I will walk out and not buy. I want the total "drive it off the lot" price.

At the time, of course, neither she nor I realized she was doing a perfect self talk routine. She was merely doing what her innate sense of business craftsmanship told her to do. At that time I had approached self talk as something one must do alone to oneself, so self talk never even entered my mind.

When we entered the dealership on that Saturday, a salesman immediately latched onto us.

My wife said, "I came to buy a car, if you are really interested in selling. I have some iron-clad ground rules, so listen carefully." She then repeated from memory all of the ground rules she had reiterated out loud to me many times every day for the preceding five days.

The salesman smiled. "No problem," he said. He then showed her three New Yorkers that met her specifications. One was blue, one grey, and one tan. She liked the blue one, and pointed out that it didn't have a full-size spare tire.

"We can get you one next week," the salesman said.

"You weren't paying attention when I laid down the rules. I drive it off the lot today exactly how I want it, or I don't buy it at all. Period!"

The salesman sort of winced and walked over to speak to some other man there. Then he returned to us. The other man scurried off, and within 15 minutes the man was back with a matching full size spare tire, which he put into the trunk of the car.

"Now what is your lowest price? Remember you have just one shot. No dickering."

The sticker price was over $22,000. The salesman said the most he could come down on his own was to $21,000 but that the sales manager could authorize more. He excused himself to go talk to the sales manager. He returned with a price of $20,000.

"You can't be serious!" my wife chided. "You aren't even close to a reasonable price. Thanks for your time. Goodbye!"

She turned abruptly to leave and bumped into a man who had just walked into the showroom.

"Is there a problem?" he asked.

"Not really. I am going to buy a car today but not here because the sales manager doesn't want to sell me that car over there." She pointed to the blue New Yorker.

"What price did the sales manager quote?" My wife told him.

The man introduced himself and added, "I own this agency. Will you give me a chance to sell you that car?"

"You have fifteen minutes. Here are the ground rules." She went over the ground rules. "Your time starts now." She looked at her watch.

"Tell you what," the owner said. "You write on a piece of paper the most you are willing to pay. I'll write on another piece of paper the least I am willing to sell the car for. If my figure matches yours or is lower than yours, you write me out a check for my figure right now and the car is yours. If my figure is higher than yours, you walk out and don't buy. No hassles. Okay?"

"We are talking total price, right?" my wife asked. "No add-on taxes or anything else?"

"Right."

"You've got a deal!"

They each wrote a figure on a sheet of paper and then played showdown. My wife had written $18,000. He had written $17,200. My wife wrote a check for $17,200 immediately and we drove off in her $22,000 plus car. A $5,000 savings.

I thought about those two experiences a lot over the next 3-1/2 years. I finally concluded that self talk was at work in both cases. I also concluded that you don't have to always be alone, just talking to yourself, to have a valid self talk session. You can talk to yourself under the appearance of talking to someone else. My wife knew that intuitively, and she knew it was effective.

I decided to put it to the test personally to either validate or invalidate my self talk theory. My car was nearly eight years old and needed about $1,000 in repairs if I was to keep it much longer. That didn't seem like a financially sound idea, so I opted to buy myself a new vehicle.

It was June, 1990. I wanted a Jeep Cherokee Laredo. I followed the exact pattern my wife had established over three years previously. I used self talk (out loud of course) to myself when alone as well as in her presence. I established my ground rules just like she had done.

Then I went to the dealer and followed my self talk script. I quickly spotted the exact car I wanted, except that it had an "emergency" spare tire instead of a regular full-size one. The sticker price was $24,000. I stuck to my programmed script.

Déjà vu! In less than two hours after walking in, I drove my Jeep out, with a full size matching spare tire, for $18,000. A $6,000 savings.

This self talk stuff really works, folks! I have validated it personally many times over.

If you are going to buy a car, follow the scenario in this chapter and you will get what you want at the price you want to pay.

Formula For Success:
Mouth Power + Word Power = Personal Power

Chapter 8

Fat City

(How to Talk Your Fat Off)

Fat is out. Lean is in. Current mores dictate that if you are heftier than a broom handle, you are fat.

I personally do not subscribe to the "be skinny" fanaticism. I am more interested in a person's heart, mind, and character than in physical dimensions. However, this chapter is not a discussion of philosophy so I will stick to the facts. We live in an anti-fat society.

There are probably as many methods to lose fat as there are fat people. So I will give you one more aid to fat reduction for your consideration—SELF TALK.

That's right, you can talk your fat off. It is slower than diet pills, but certainly safer. It is faster than doing nothing.

Talking your fat off works at its best when used in conjunction with a sensible diet. It will work faster than just dieting without the self talk. This is the approach I will present in this chapter.

In showing you how to lose weight via self talk, I will employ a sample diet to give you the idea of combining the diet with the self talk.

The diet I use is for illustration only, and I do not imply that it is the specific diet that is best for you. It is only an example.

Selecting a proper diet is a serious matter, and you should consult your health professional and use your own good sense in making the selection. I am not a diet expert (except for myself) and I am not a health professional.

What I am an expert at is in showing you how to use self talk in conjunction with your own dieting program to make that program even more successful.

Now here is how it works. The diet I will use in this chapter is given on the following page.

BREAKFAST
Small serving of protein (2-3 ounces)
Small serving of fruit or juice (4 ounces)
One piece of unbuttered toast

LUNCH
Small serving of protein (3-4 ounces)
Small serving of fresh fruit or vegetable

DINNER
Small serving of protein (4-5 ounces)
Small salad with light dressing
Half cup of cooked vegetable served without
    butter
Diet drinks, except colas, are okay
Decaffeinated coffee only
No gravies or sauces

This amounts to approximately 800 to 1000 calories per day

You may substitute your own diet in place of this one if you wish.

The self talk approach will be to say your diet out loud before each meal along with some supportive statements. Then after each meal again say some supportive statements out loud. I'll take you through a complete sample cycle in a few moments.

Using Self Talk with your diet

There are good reasons for using self talk in conjunction with your diet.

First: Most diets fail because people do not stick to them faithfully. Self talk is a self-disciplining mechanism that tends to help you stick with the diet program.

Second: As you know by now from the preceding chapters, self talk is a powerful reinforcement mechanism for achieving any goal.

The dieting self talk program gives you a triple whammy.

1. You tell yourself out loud what you are going to eat and why. This sets your mind up for receptiveness to your diet plan.

2. Then you eat the diet meal that you have just described. This satisfies your mind's goal seeking quest, and it also reinforces your self talk and your diet commitment.

3. Finally you tell yourself out loud what you have just done and why you have done it. This is powerful reinforcement for the first two steps.

In combination, these three steps get you off the "fat" track and onto the "lean" track quickly, effectively, and in a healthy manner.

About now you are wondering how you are going to say your self talk routine out loud before and after meals because you often eat in the presence of other people.

No problem. Let's examine the three possible eating scenarios: by yourself; with your family; with non-family members.

Eating by yourself is no problem at all. You just talk out loud to yourself as prescribed in the scenario that I will present shortly.

Eating with your family members gives you two options. The first option is to let them in on what you are doing so they can be supportive. It will be sort of a game, and they can help keep you on track. You just talk out loud to yourself at the table. They won't think anything of it because they are in on it. If you do not wish to use the first option, then just go into another room for a few minutes before and after the meal to do your self talk. The bathroom is always a good choice because you know you will have privacy.

When eating with non-family members (restaurant, at work, etc.), just go to the restroom and occupy one of the booths for a few moments. You can talk softly (a whisper) and no one will know.

The important thing is to be sure to do the self talk every time as prescribed as part of your diet program. Hit and miss doesn't cut it—you must be dedicated.

Here is the sample scenario:

Breakfast

Before eating, say out loud: "In a few moments I am going to eat a healthy breakfast consisting of one poached egg on a piece of toast, one strip of crisp bacon, and a four ounce glass of orange juice. This breakfast will give me all the nourishment I need just now, and it will also fill me up. This breakfast will help me to lose excess weight in a sensible way until I reach my desired weight. When I reach my desired weight, I will then maintain that weight by continuing to eat sensibly."

EAT YOUR BREAKFAST

After breakfast, say out loud: "I have just eaten a nourishing breakfast that will help me lose excess weight. I will not eat any food between meals. If I get hungry between meals I will drink water, which is healthy and will fill me up."

Lunch

Before eating, say out loud: "In a few moments I am going to eat a healthy lunch, consisting of one four ounce broiled hamburger patty and a small serving of applesauce. This lunch will give me all the nourishment I need just now, and it will also fill me up. This lunch will help me to lose excess weight in a sensible way until I reach my desired weight. When I reach my desired weight, I will then maintain that weight by continuing to eat sensibly."

EAT YOUR LUNCH

After lunch, say out loud: "I have just eaten a nourishing lunch that will help me lose excess weight. I will not eat any food between meals. If I get hungry between meals I will drink water, which is healthy and will fill me up."

Dinner

Before eating, say out loud: "In a few moments I am going to eat a healthy dinner consisting of a baked chicken breast half, a small lettuce salad with light dressing, a half cup of sauteed zucchini, and a cup of black decaffeinated coffee. This dinner will give me all the nourishment I need just now, and it will also fill me up. This dinner will help me to lose excess weight in a sensible way until I reach my desired weight. When I reach my desired weight, I will then maintain that weight by continuing to eat sensibly."

EAT YOUR DINNER

After dinner, say out loud: "I have just eaten a nourishing dinner that will help me lose excess weight. I will not eat any food between meals. If I get hungry between meals I will drink water, which is healthy and will fill me up."

Of course, you should substitute the description of the food you are actually going to eat in place of the food I used in the preceding example.

That is all there is to it. If you follow this scenario faithfully every day, you will lose the excess fat. Nothing could be simpler. You literally talk your fat off.

Formula For Success:
Mouth Power + Word Power = Personal Power

Chapter 9

Hi There, Chimney Mouth!

(Self Talk vs Smoking)

Nearly every smoker I know alleges that he/she wants to stop smoking. "Someday I am going to quit." "I know it isn't good for me and I should quit." "The doctor says my smoking is harmful to my baby, but . . . ." And so it goes.

It isn't that smokers are not aware of all the negatives involved with smoking. They know that their breath smells like the inside of a chimney in a coal-fired power plant. Their clothes stink. Their hair stinks. Their smoke impregnates the clothing of other people, making them stink. The room in which they smoke stinks.

And more importantly, they know that the smoke harms their health and the health of others.

They know that lungs were designed to take in clean air and expel harmful air. And yet they deliberately force their lungs to take in harmful air. It doesn't make sense, does it?

It would take an extremely stupid person to believe that smoking was not a totally hazardous and unintelligent habit. Yet smokers are not stupid people. They are intelligent, creative, worthwhile people.

So what is the problem? Why do intelligent people aggressively pursue an unintelligent activity?

In my opinion, they seem to have done a "con job" on themselves. They have made themselves believe in the unbelievable.

If you stand on a railroad track in the presence of an oncoming train, and you don't move, you will be killed. That is believable. To think that the train will miss you is unbelievable. Yet smokers seem to have convinced themselves that the train won't hit them.

Part of the problem is that smoking tends to be addictive—more so in some people than in others. The other part of the problem has to do with our mind's ability to make us believe what we choose to believe, regardless of whether the belief is valid or not.

There are a variety of products on the market that supposedly help a person stop smoking. These products' success rate, according to my personal observation, ranges from marginally successful to unsuccessful because they only address the addictive nature of smoking.

This tells me that the mental nature of smoking is by far the most powerful influence. I believe that if smokers change their mental state with regard to smoking, most would become non-smokers quickly, without needing the various products that deal with the addictive aspect. The heavily addicted smokers would probably benefit from the "stop smoking" products if used in conjunction with a self-induced mental change.

I deliberately use the term "self-induced mental change" because I am convinced that the smoker is the only one who can make himself/herself stop smoking. Any mind that is powerful enough to make one believe that the oncoming train won't hit them is powerful enough to make them realize that it will hit them and impel them to get out of the way. Smoking is a self-induced habit, and it has a self-induced solution. Becoming a non-smoker is a self-induced habit.

I am a professional hypnotherapist, and I have dealt with many smokers who allegedly wanted to quit smoking. That experience validates everything I am writing in this chapter.

Smokers are the only ones who can effectively stop themselves. No one else can do it for them. There is no magic pill. Smokers must reprogram their own minds to see the oncoming train realistically.

This is where self talk comes in. Self talk gives you a specific tool to use on yourself to make yourself become a non-smoker.

In a moment I will give you a suggested self talk re-programming procedure. You may use it as is, or you may alter the wording if you choose. In any case, you must read your daily self talk out loud to yourself as prescribed.

First, you must be serious about wanting to stop smoking. If you are doing this because your spouse wants you to stop but you really don't want to stop, you have an excellent chance for failure.

So think about this. Reread this chapter a few times. Then make up your own mind.

When you have made up your own mind, select a date to start. Preferably, it should be the same day you made up your mind, but no longer than one week away. If you are stalling for more than a week, you aren't serious. Get a calendar you can mark up to keep track of your successful progress.

Circle your starting day on the calendar and label it "START." Now you are ready to proceed.

Non-Smoking Self Talk Program

1st day

You will be allowed to continue smoking this first day only, but I do urge you to exercise willpower to reduce the amount you smoke.

When you get up in the morning, stand in front of your bathroom mirror, look yourself in the eyes, and say out loud to yourself the following words *three times:*

"Today is the last day I will smoke tobacco in any form."

At day's end, while smoking your final smoke, read the following out loud to yourself *three times:*

"This is the last time I will smoke tobacco in any form. I am making a commitment to myself to become a non-smoker from the moment I finish this smoke, and I never go back on my commitments. When I awaken tomorrow morning I will be a confirmed non-smoker."

After you finish this last smoke, immediately destroy all remaining tobacco you have. Tear it up! Crush it! Throw it in the trash can, never to be retrieved.

Then put an "X" through that day on your calendar to signify success. Go to bed feeling good about your accomplishment.

2nd day

From this day throughout the rest of this self talk program, ask others to not smoke in your house, your car, and your office. Explain to them that it will help you achieve your goal. They will be happy to oblige. After you complete the program, you may continue with this request if you wish. From now on always sit in the non-smoking section of restaurants. This is important reinforcement for your self talk program.

When you get up in the morning, stand in front of your bathroom mirror, look yourself in the eyes, and say out loud the following words to yourself *three times:*

"Yesterday I stopped using tobacco forever. I am a non-smoker and proud of it."

Sometime during the evening, read the following out loud to yourself:

"I have now completed my first full day without using tobacco. This is how it is going to be every day for the rest of my life, because this is what I want. I am proud of myself for being a non-smoker."

Then cross off another successful day on your calendar.

3rd day through 30th day

For each day from day three through day thirty, do the following when you go into the bathroom in the morning. Look into the mirror and say out loud,

"Hi there, non-smoker. I'm proud of you for not smoking."

Then sometime during the day, at your choosing, read the following out loud to yourself. You may read it more often than once a day if you wish, but just once is required. Any time during the day is fine, and just before bedtime is especially good.

"I have succeeded in being a non-smoker for another day. I have chosen to be a non-smoker for many reasons. I know smoking is harmful to my health, and since I only have one life to live I want to live it in the best health I possibly can. I know that smoking makes me stink, and I have too much self respect to want to be a dirty and smelly person. I know that smoking can be harmful and unpleasant to others, and I have no right to inflict harm or unpleasantness on others. And perhaps most importantly, I know that if I smoke I am turning control of some portion of my life over to a few ounces of dried tobacco leaves instead of controlling my entire life myself. It just doesn't make sense for an intelligent person to allow a few ounces of dried leaves to make major decisions concerning their health and self-esteem. Therefore, I have permanently declared myself to be a non-smoker. I have taken total control of my life, and that is the way it will be from now on. I like myself and am proud of myself for this decision. I like being a non-smoker."

At the end of each day, cross off one more day as a successful day on your calendar.

After the thirtieth day, read the statement out loud to yourself once a week for six more weeks. After that you can stop the self talk if you wish, or you can do it occasionally if you feel the need.

This may seem like a long self talk program to you, but it will go fast. After all, you programmed yourself to be a smoker over many months or years. You are now turning that around in quite a short time. Your mind is powerful enough to do it. You only need to tell your mind what you want, using self talk.

During the period of days for your non-smoking self talk programming you may have the urge to smoke. You can combat those urges with self talk, chewing gum, chewing a toothpick, or forcing yourself to get involved in some activity so your mind will be pulled away from the smoking urge.

Getting an urge does not mean the program isn't working. The program is working, but your mind may rebel for a while, just like a recalcitrant child who has been told to stop doing something that he wants to do.

You don't give in and let a child do something that can be harmful such as playing on the railroad tracks, do you? Of course you don't. So don't give into your mind's urges to want to play on the railroad tracks (continuing to smoke) either. Don't stand there and let the train run you down. Instead, get out of the train's path—stop smoking by using self talk!

Formula For Success:
Mouth Power + Word Power = Personal Power

Chapter 10

When Life Gives
You a Lemon

(Self Talk Constructive Affirmations)

The entire self talk concept and practice that I describe in this book began for me in early 1972. At that time, I started giving myself daily constructive affirmations for my benefit in general. What got me started on this was the work of the French psychotherapist Emile Coue (1857-1926). Coue instructed his patients to say to themselves every day, "Every day in every way I am getting better and better."

And, indeed, Coue's patients did get better and better. So I thought, "Why not me?" I started saying Coue's short, constructive affirmation out loud to myself every day, usually when I was driving my car.

Coue's affirmation is a sort of generic, all-encompassing statement so I didn't know specifically what, if anything, to expect. Within just a few weeks my life began to change profoundly. Unexpected things happened—like losing my job after eighteen years service. In retrospect, losing that job was one of the best things that ever happened to me. At the time, however, it seemed traumatic. That event opened up other possibilities. I kept moving in a direction of greater self-fulfillment, greater prosperity, and greater happiness.

Concurrently with all these changes, I began to develop additional constructive affirmations and included them in my daily self talk. At first they were generic statements also, such as: "Positive thoughts benefit me," "I am in control of my own life," and "I am expanding all my abilities."

Soon, however, I began using affirmations for specific situations. Some of my affirmations became quite extensive and I had to write them down and read them. I borrowed the words of others for much of my affirmation material. I borrowed words and concepts from the Bible, Shakespeare, Jose Silva, Lincoln, Omar Khayyam, and other renowned sources. I also borrowed heavily from wise sayings and proverbs whose authorship is unknown.

For example, the saying, "If life hands you a lemon, make lemonade," was one I used to develop the following constructive affirmation when I was out of work.

"Life has given me a lemon—I lost my job. I am going to make lemonade by finding an exciting, rewarding new career path that is more beneficial to me than anything I have ever done before."

After just a few days of repeating the above "lemon" affirmation out loud to myself, I got the idea that I would like to become a hypnotherapist because I was greatly impressed by the work of Emile Coue and of Jose Silva. But I didn't know how to go about it, so I continued repeating the affirmation.

A couple of days later I got a flash idea to look up a hypnotherapist in the phone book and then go and apply for an apprenticeship, not knowing whether this sort of thing was done or not.

The phone book listed several dozen hypnotists and hypnotherapists. So before making a selection, I gave myself the following self talk affirmation for several days.

"On next Thursday I am going to select a hypnotherapist from the phone book for me to interview with, and my selection will be the best possible choice for me."

On Thursday I opened the phone book and began reading each hypnotist listing slowly out loud. On one particular name, a quiet awareness of "This is the one" flashed into my mind. It was a woman whom I will call Amy Smith to protect her privacy.

For several more days prior to visiting Ms. Smith, I gave myself the following affirmation:

"When I visit Amy Smith next Monday, I will be confident and relaxed. I will do and say exactly the right things to impress her so much that she will hire me as a trainee."

That Monday was a major turning point in my life. Ms. Smith interviewed me in great depth. In her words, "Even though you don't have a degree in psychology or in anything related, your technical and practical knowledge and your people skills far exceed anything I would expect to find in someone with a recent doctorate in psychology. You are hired." I should point out that I read extensively and I have a superb memory, with a high retention level for everything I've read.

Ms. Smith trained me, got me certified as a hypnotherapist, and got me started on that exciting, rewarding, and beneficial career path that I had programmed myself for with self talk.

As a hypnotherapist I became acutely aware of the power of the spoken word. That led me to continue to expand the scope of my self talk concept. This book is testimony to that work. I have gone far beyond mere constructive affirmations as you can see, but constructive affirmations is where it all started.

Early in my career as a hypnotherapist, I created the following lengthy affirmation for myself. Initially, I read it to myself out loud once a day for a month, then once a week for several years. Now I read it out loud as a reinforcement affirmation about four or five times a year. This has been an extremely powerful self talk session for me, which I will elaborate on shortly. Feel free to use it yourself or modify it to suit your specific situation as you choose. Or perhaps just use it as a model from which you construct your own powerful self talk session.

Affirmation Script

The words I am reading and speaking are an affirmation of who I am, what I am doing and will continue to do in this life, and my goals and desires. This is truth . . . This is reality, and this is so. The full power, scope and meaning of these words and the thought behind them are recorded permanently and indestructibly in my entire being and at every level of my consciousness. These words and their accompanying thoughts create the reality of me in this life experience identified as William Wayne Hewitt. Every time I say these words, hear these words, read these words, or think these words or have any allied thoughts related to these words, the reality of the me, the self, expressed by the words becomes infinitely more powerful, more immediate, and more effective in every facet of my reality and experience.

I am one of God's children . . . one of His sons, and as such am a residence of His divine powers and divine presence. I do His work with honor, success, distinction, and integrity in whatever ways He gives me the awareness to serve. This prayer by St. Francis of Assisi expresses my service to God:

Lord, make me an instrument of Thy
    Peace.
Where there is hatred, let me sow love.
Where there is injury, pardon.
Where there is doubt, faith.
Where there is despair, hope.
Where there is darkness, light.
Where there is sadness, joy.

O Divine Master, grant that I may not so
    much seek to be consoled as to console;
    to be understood, as to understand; to
    be loved, as to love; for it is in giving
    that we receive, it is in pardoning that
    we are pardoned, and it is in dying that
    we are born to Eternal Life.

My powers of visualization are clear, good, powerful, and effective for the good of all and with harm to no one.

I have the power to completely heal self of all imbalances, infirmities, illnesses, disorders and discords in my entire being . . . spiritually, physically, mentally, and emotionally. As a result, I am in perfect health and balance at every level of my being physically, mentally, spiritually, and emotionally. I also have the power and ability to be an effective healing agent for others. I bring about healing in others by triggering their own self-healing powers into effective action and by directing to others the infinite healing powers of the universe that are channeled through me for that purpose. All healing comes from God; I act merely as an agent or catalyst for focusing that healing in self and others.

My destiny is to serve God and humanity with honor, success, and distinction in the public light as a public figure, a teacher, a lecturer, a writer, a healer, an astrologer, a hypnotherapist, a psychic, and as a personality using all my God-given talents, skills, and abilities for the good of mankind. I am already doing this, and each day I do more and more with ever increasing success in every respect . . . benefiting individuals and nations . . . benefiting self in spiritual growth and financial growth . . . I am gaining an ever increasing conscious awareness and enlightenment in every respect, with harm to no one and with benefit for everyone.

My every thought and action are guided by truth, wisdom, and love from Higher Mind which is perfect and divine.

I am severing my servitude to corporations and man-made institutions. I am channeling all my energies in servitude only to God for the benefit of humanity and for the enrichment of self at every level of self.

All the money and material wealth and blessings I ever want or need are always mine . . . even more than I need is always mine so that I may share with others. I am never in want for anything I need. I claim my wealth, blessings, and enrichment at every level of my existence from the infinite bounty of God which is available to all who ask and claim it.

I am financially independent. I am physically sound and capable. I am mentally alert, intelligent, and wise. I am emotionally stable and mature. I am spiritually in tune with God.

I am a success. I am a winner. I am God's son. I am an instrument through whom God expresses himself to the world. I am.

Just one example to show the power of the preceding self talk affirmation: When I created it, I had not written a book of any kind. I didn't even know what I would, or could, write about. Today I have five successful books and fifteen tape cassettes on the market. Some of the books have already been translated into other languages, and other prospective translations are in the works. I have two booklets completed and in the process of being published as I write this book. And this book you are now reading is my sixth. I have dozens more in my mind to write.

In addition to the books, many other aspects of this self talk affirmation have already materialized and other aspects are in the process of materializing. Already materialized: lecturer, writer, healer, astrologer, hypnotherapist, psychic. In the process of materializing: financial wealth and independence, even greater psychic development, becoming a public figure, spiritual growth.

Are words powerful? Is self talk powerful? I think you know the answer. Make the magic happen for yourself now.

The balance of this chapter consists of some material that might be beneficial to you in developing your own constructive affirmations. Some of you may want to use this material as is. Others may want to use a concept from which you develop an affirmation, just as I did with the "lemon" saying. Start the habit of writing down or memorizing quotations and ideas from every source. At some time they can be valuable to you in your practice of self talk.

These are just a small sampling of all the material I have drawn on at one time or the other, and still do draw on. I find this material helps me keep my head screwed on straight, keep my perspective in balance, and enables me to continually progress in every avenue of my life.

In the material that follows I furnish the source where known.

Self Talk Affirmation Source Material

On goal setting and achievement

- The following is my paraphrasing of an ancient Chinese philosophy:

  I am learning to be orderly in my life,
  To see the end of things at the beginning,
  To not take action until I foresee the
     outcome of my action,
  And to approach the realization of my
     goals with caution.

- The following is attributed to President Calvin Coolidge:

  Press on. Nothing in the world can take the place of persistence. Talent will not; nothing is more common than unsuccessful people with talent. Genius will not; unrewarded genius is almost a proverb. Education alone will not; the world is full of educated derelicts. Persistence and determination alone are omnipotent.

- From me:

  There are many excellent ways to achieve failure, but not taking a chance is the most successful. I will, therefore, take a chance on myself and I will not fail. Instead I will succeed in everything I set my mind and energies on. I will never give up, but will always press on with courage and faith in myself.

- From *The Winds of Fate* by Ella Wheeler Wilcox (1850-1919):

  One ship drives east and another drives
    west
  With the selfsame winds that blow.
  `Tis the set of the sails
  And not the gales
  Which tells us the way to go.
  Like the winds of the sea are the ways of
    fate,
  As we voyage along through life:
  `Tis the set of a soul
  That decides its goal
  And not the calm or the strife.

- From Pamela Vaull Starr:

  Reach high, for stars lie hidden in your soul. Dream deep, for every dream precedes the goal.

On personal achievement

- Unknown author:

  I shall pass through this world but once. Any good therefore that I can do or any kindness that I can show to any human being, let me do it now. Let me not defer or neglect it, for I shall not pass this way again.

- From Henry Ward Beecher:

  God asks no man whether he will accept life. That is not the choice. You must take it. The only choice is how.

- From Emile Coue, with an additional "better" which I added because I have a penchant for doing things in threes:

  Every day in every way I am getting better, better, and better.

- From "A Warrior's Prayer," unknown author:

  I am what I am.
  In having faith in the beauty within me I
    develop trust.
  In softness I have strength.
  In silence I walk with the Gods.
  In peace I understand myself and the
    world.
  In conflict I walk away.
  In detachment I am free.
  In respecting all living things I respect
    myself.

  In dedication I honor the courage within
    me.
  In eternity I have compassion for the
    nature of all things.
  In love I unconditionally accept the
    evolution of others.
  In freedom I have power.
  In my individuality I express the God
    force within me.
  In service I give what I have become.
  I am what I am: Eternal, Immortal,
    Universal, and Infinite and so be it.

- From me:

  I have full control over all my faculties at
  all times.

- Author unknown:

  If life hands you a lemon, make lemonade.

- Author unknown:

  If I am not for me, who will be? If I am for only me, who am I? If not now, when?

- From me:

  I have but one life to live, and I shall live it with honor, success, distinction, and integrity.

- From Harry Emerson Fosdick:

  Most of us can afford to take a lesson from the oyster. The most extraordinary thing about the oyster is this. Irritations get into its shell. It does not like them; it tries to get rid of them. But when it cannot get rid of them, it settles down to make of them one of the most beautiful things in the world. It uses the irritation to do the loveliest thing that an oyster ever has a chance to do. If there are irritations in your life today, there is only one prescription: make a pearl. It may have to be a pearl of patience, but, anyhow, make a pearl. And it takes faith and love to do it.

On maintaining perspective about life

- From *Ecclesiastes*:

  *To every thing there is a season, and a time
  to every purpose under the heaven.
  A time to be born, and a time to die; a time
  to plant, and a time to pluck up that
  which has been planted;
  A time to kill, and a time to heal; a time to
  break down, and a time to build up;
  A time to weep, and a time to laugh; a
  time to mourn, and a time to dance;
  A time to cast away stones, and a time to
  gather stones together; a time to embrace,
  and a time to refrain from embracing;
  A time to get, and a time to lose; a time to
  keep, and a time to cast away;
  A time to rend, and a time to sew; a time
  to keep silence, and a time to speak;
  A time to love, and a time to hate; a time of
  war, and a time of peace.*

At the end of this, I always add, "And there is a
time for me, and I believe my time is now."

- From the *Rubaiyat of Omar Khayyam*:

  *The moving finger writes; and, having
  writ, Moves on: nor all your piety nor wit
  Shall call it back to cancel half a line, Nor
  all your tears wash out a word of it.*

- My paraphrasing of some words Edward FitzGerald wrote in the mid-1800s about the philosophy of Omar Khayyam:

  I am not worried about tomorrow. Tomorrow has not come. Tomorrow may never come. There is only today, and today is mine.

On overcoming the "blues"

- From me:

  Life may be tough, but it sure beats the alternative. The sun always comes out after the storm.

On dealing with problems

- From Shakespeare's "*Julius Caesar*, Act II, Scene II:

  *Cowards die many times before their
      death;
  The valiant never taste of death but once.
  Of all the wonders I yet have heard,
  It seems to me most strange that men
      should fear;
  Seeing that death, a necessary end,
  Will come when it will come.*

- From me:

  *No matter what happens, I can handle it in
  a sensible, mature, and beneficial manner.
  Forewarned is half armed.*

- From "What Is Dying?", author unknown:

  *I am standing on the seashore, and a ship
  at my side spreads her white sails to the
  morning breeze and sets out for the blue
  ocean. She is an object of beauty and
  strength, and I stand and watch her until
  at length she hangs like a speck out there
  where the sky and water seem to mingle
  with each other. At that moment, someone
  at my side says, "There, she's gone."*

  *Gone? Gone where? Gone from my sight
  that is all. For she is just as large in mast
  and hull and spar as she was when she left
  my side, and just as able to carry her load
  of living freight to the point of destination. Her diminished size is in me, not in
  her. For at that moment when someone at
  my side had said, "There, she's gone,"
  there were other eyes watching her coming and other voices ready to take up the
  glad shout, "There! She comes!" And that
  is dying.*

On personal faith

- From the 23rd Psalm:

  The Lord is my shepherd, and I shall not want. He maketh me to lie down in green pastures. He leadeth me beside the still waters. He restoreth my soul. He leadeth me on the paths of righteousness for His namesake. And yea though I walk through the valley of the shadow of death, I shall fear no evil for thou art with me. Thy rod and thy staff, they comfort me. Thou preparest a table before me in the presence of my enemies. Thou anointest my head with oil. My cup runneth over. Surely goodness and mercy shall follow me all the days of my life, and I shall dwell in the house of the Lord forever.

Formula For Success:
Mouth Power + Word Power = Personal Power

Chapter 11

Hire Me!

(Prepare for a Job Interview with Self Talk)

Interviewing for a job is an experience most of us have at least once, and usually many times, in our life. And if you are typical, it isn't an experience you look forward to. Also, if you are typical, your interviews weren't always successful—there were times when you didn't get the job.

Self talk can help you better prepare yourself for an interview, thus increasing your chances for getting the job.

Before I get into interviewing self talk, let me digress for a moment to briefly cover some other aspects of interviewing. The reason I mention these other aspects is because if you "bomb out" on these, all the self talk in the world may not save the day for you.

You have heard the adage, "You never get a second chance to make a first impression." Your first impression is the one that will permeate the entire interview. Make a good first impression, and it will cancel out some minor goof-ups you might make during the interview. Make a bad first impression, and it will cancel out many of the excellent things you might say during the interview.

Tips on making a good first impression:

1. Be on time for the interview. Being fifteen minutes ahead of time is even better because it gives you time to fill out any forms the prospective employer may want.

2. Be neat and clean. You don't have to dress like a fashion model (there are a few exceptions to this), but you must have on clean, pressed clothing. Nothing too radical, such as beach clothing. Just use good taste, and perhaps lean toward the conservative side.

3. Take care of your personal hygiene. No body odor or dragon breath. There is no excuse in our society for not complying with this requirement.

4. Don't smoke unless the interviewer volunteers an invitation to do so. If the interviewer smokes, then you may also.

I spent many years in management with IBM, and I interviewed countless numbers of people. I had some interviewees who flagrantly violated the first three rules. Three cases that come to mind are:

1. An electrical engineer showed up an hour and a half late for a 10:30 a.m. appointment because he "overslept." He didn't bother to phone either.

2. A woman showed up in a see-through blouse. She wasn't wearing a bra.

3. A man showed up reeking of body odor so strong I could smell him before I could see him. When he got close enough to speak, his breath was even more foul than his body.

None of these three people got hired. I personally have not had anyone violate rule number four, probably because I had a prominent NO SMOKING sign in my office.

Forewarned is half-armed. Follow the preceding four rules to make a good first impression.

Now let's assume you will comply with the preceding rules. What else do you need to do? You need to convince the interviewer that you are the one he/she needs to hire.

This is where self talk comes in. With self talk you can prepare yourself to have a successful interview. In short, self talk can help you sell yourself.

One caution—self talk will not help much if you have no qualifications for the job. If the employer wants to hire an experienced carpenter and you have never even held a hammer in your hand, self talk isn't likely to get you hired. So for self talk, I will assume that you are already somewhat qualified for the job.

Even when you are qualified, you can bomb out by excessive nervousness, lack of self-confidence, talking too much, not talking enough, displaying a negative or defeatist attitude, or by not showing sincere interest or enthusiasm.

Sample self talk session

You can deal with the "bombs" in the preceding paragraph by a few simple self talks prior to going for the interview. The self talk session I am now going to give you is sort of generic. You may want to tailor it to suit your specific situation. If you have several days before the interview, read the self talk out loud at least twice a day, every day. If you have only one day, or only a few hours notice, use it at least three times if you possibly can.

"On (state the date and time) I am going to be interviewed for (state the specific job/purpose).

"During the interview, I will be relaxed and calm. I am confident that I can fill the job with excellence, and I shall display my confidence.

"I will talk easily and comfortably and I will answer all questions honestly and fully.

"I will listen attentively and will ask questions about the job and the company. I will balance my talking and listening to about fifty-fifty.

"Here are my qualifications and what I have to offer the employer:"

(Here you will state what qualifies you for the job and why you are the right person for the job).

"Here are some questions I definitely want to ask at the interview:"

(Here state the specific questions you want the interviewer to answer for you).

The preceding self talk session is quite simple and to the point. In essence, it is a mock interview. So pretend you are being interviewed when you talk to yourself. Put some enthusiasm and drama into your words when you state your qualifications and do your "selling" job. Convince the invisible interviewer that he/she should hire you. The more enthusiasm you can work up the better because the words will make an even deeper impression on your mind.

The more "dry runs" you make with a self talk session such as this, the greater the chances of your making a good, solid impression on the interviewer when you have the actual interview.

This self talk session "preps" you. It impregnates your mind with the thoughts and facts that you want to prevail during the interview. Then when you get into the actual interview you don't have the stress of trying to think fast about what to do or say because it is already in your mind. The result is that your interview will be more like a casual conversation between two friends.

Actors and actresses seem so natural in their roles because they have practiced their role many times before their actual performance.

An interview is a performance, and you are the actor or actress. Use self talk first to give you practice, then you will give an award-winning performance. Your award: YOU WILL BE HIRED!

Formula For Success:
Mouth Power + Word Power = Personal Power

Chapter 12

I Am OK—You Are Not OK

(Self Talk Tune-up on Prejudice)

Two of the dictionary's definitions for prejudice are:

1. The act or state of holding unreasonable preconceived judgements or convictions.

2. A preconceived preference or idea.

The first definition above is an insidious malignancy that is pervasive in all societies and nations in the world today.

Hitler and Stalin's prejudice against Jews resulted in the inexcusable slaughter of millions of innocent, decent human beings.

Prejudice against blacks in America caused, and is still causing, death, social imprisonment, and subjugation of millions of innocent, decent human beings.

Religious prejudice in Ireland has been causing death and destruction for years there, and the end doesn't seem to be in sight.

Bias against women deprives them of wages, treatment, and considerations they deserve.

And so it goes. It seems most of us are in a minority group of some sort. And being in a minority group seems to qualify one to be a candidate for prejudice by someone else. Here are some of the prominent minority groups: religion, race, nationality, age (seniors and teenagers especially), geographical location, skin color, educational level, political beliefs, family name, occupation, financial status, gender, sexual preference, and disabilities. Within those groups there are often subgroups of minorities. For example, within the Protestant religions there are many diverse sects, each of which may harbor prejudice against other Protestant sects.

Prejudice destroys nations and societies. It destroys families. It destroys individuals. It is senseless and needless.

There is something each of us individually can do about it. We can make a concerted effort to keep ourselves in balance and free of prejudice. We can use self talk to tune ourselves up so destructive prejudice does not become a part of our thoughts and actions.

Each person who keeps him/herself tuned up against personal prejudice pulls one tooth from the jaws of the giant monster of social prejudice. If enough people pull teeth, the giant will loose its biting and chewing ability and thus starve to death. In a few moments I will furnish you with a simple self talk exercise that will help you pull one of those teeth.

But first, let's examine the second definition of prejudice: "A preconceived preference or idea." Within the scope of this definition there is room for a positive, constructive kind of prejudice.

There is a strong need in society for a powerful prejudice against greed, crime, drunken driving, unjustified violence against any human or creature (the key here is "unjustified" because we do have a right to be violent in self-defense or to defend someone else). In short, we should be prejudiced against anything that unjustly deprives another human being or creature of their rights.

With self talk we can create this good kind of prejudice within ourselves. In so doing, we strengthen our own character and contribute to a stronger, better society.

Most of us really don't believe we are prejudiced against other groups of people. I know I don't think I am. But we are usually mistaken about this. It is hard to be absolutely certain under all circumstances.

So let's not take chances. Let's keep ourselves tuned up "just in case." It only takes a few minutes, and it can make us and society stronger and better. I frequently give myself these tune-ups.

Let's destroy "bad" prejudice and replace it with "good" prejudice by using self talk. Here is a suggested generic self talk program to do just that. As with all self talk programs, you may alter it to suit your specific situation. Do this self talk program as often as you wish. I suggest at least once a month. If prejudice is a problem with you, do the program daily until you get "tuned-up."

Read the following out loud to yourself. I wholeheartedly encourage family and group participation in this.

- I respect the rights and beliefs of all people without exception, as long as their actions do not deprive others of their rights.

- I vow to never do or say anything detrimental to the rights of any other person or groups of people.

- I shall strive to learn more about people and groups who are different than me so I can better understand them and thus be able to better respect them and to harmonize with them.

- Whenever I encounter prejudice, I shall do whatever I can to counteract it.

- By keeping myself tuned up against personal prejudice, I am pulling a tooth from the jaws of the giant monster of social prejudice.

- Here are some good prejudices that I am making a part of my character. I am prejudiced against greed, crime, drunken driving, social

injustice, and unjustified violence. I am prejudiced against any word or action that deprives
another human being of their rights.

• I extend my thoughts and actions to embrace
  all creatures."

Formula For Success:
Mouth Power + Word Power = Personal Power

Chapter 13

Shut Up, You Old War Horse

(Self Talk for Spouses)

Probably the most difficult situation for any person to deal with successfully is an emotionally charged disagreement with their spouse.

Have you ever felt like screaming "Shut up you old war horse! You don t know what you are talking about!" or some similar set of words during a disagreement with your spouse?

Or perhaps you have actually screamed some such harsh remark at your spouse. If you have, you know where it got you—nowhere pleasant. Such emotional remarks merely escalate the emotional intensity to a higher decibel level and to a lower level of intelligent communication. When emotion enters, intelligence leaves.

The very nature of marriage (or any other close relationship) invites disagreements from time to time. Disagreements are normal, and are beneficial when handled in a loving, mature, and rational manner. They are beneficial because they enable each person to better understand their mate and themself. Disagreements often help to solve problems.

However, when disagreements are not handled in a loving, mature, and rational manner they can become extremely harmful and destructive to both parties. Disagreements that evolve into screaming matches, vile accusations, nasty remarks, or even into physical violence are always harmful and destructive. The participants degrade their own humanity to that of a banshee, and they do great harm to their own self-esteem as well as to their spouse's self-esteem.

A banshee is a spirit in Gaelic folklore who predicts an impending death in the family by screaming and wailing. In like manner, those in a relationship who scream and shout harsh remarks are predicting the death of that relationship.

So you can see that the business of handling disagreements is a very serious matter indeed.

There are some self-proclaimed experts today who promote open confrontation as a solution to disagreements. They say that we should say exactly what we think and feel without regard to the other person's feelings. They promote face-to-face screaming matches as a solution to problems.

I recently saw a television show where one of these so-called experts showed videos of confrontations between husbands and wives that he encouraged in his clients. The abusive, degrading language was horrible. Knowing that it was for real—not actors playing a part—made it difficult to watch.

The actual participants were then interviewed by the "expert." The "expert" asked each one the same question, "How did it make you feel to get your anger and frustration off your chest?" Each participant said that they felt good about getting everything off their chest.

"There, you see," the expert said, "this is really good therapy."

The show's host apparently wasn't buying it and asked, "Are all of you now happily married?"

One hundred percent of them answered that they got divorced shortly after the encounter shown on the video. One woman said that even though she felt good about getting things off her chest, she was deeply hurt by her husband's remarks to her. So hurt, that she said that is what caused the divorce. "I could never forget those terrible things he said to me."

"I didn't mean it the way it sounded," he defended. "I was just letting off steam like you were."

Then the other participants chimed in to say they felt exactly the same way—they enjoyed letting off steam, but were deeply hurt by their spouse's remarks.

The host gave the "expert" a glance that said, "Who are you trying to fool? This stuff is harmful, not helpful." Then there was a commercial break. After the commercials, a different subject was discussed with some other guest, so I turned the television set off.

The "expert's" claim to fame was that he had a doctor's degree, and, by inference, was infallible.

I disagree 100% with this "expert's" approach to solving personal disagreements. Having a Ph.D. degree does not, in and of itself, qualify a person for anything. In matters of personal counselling, common sense and a caring heart are much more important—two things the "expert" lacked.

The truth is quite evident. Words are extremely powerful, and once they are spoken they cannot be retrieved or cancelled. Whenever you speak to someone or to yourself, choose your words wisely.

For example, there is a world of difference between saying, "You are stupid!" and "You behaved in a stupid manner at the party last night!"

In the first statement you are assaulting a person's self esteem and telling him he has a serious defect that makes him an unacceptable human being.

In the second statement you are reminding him that he temporarily behaved in an undesirable manner that is not his usual behavior pattern. There is no assault on his worth as a human being.

The first statement drives a permanent wedge between you and the other person. The second statement does not.

What this is all leading up to is self talk. I have a recommended self talk scenario for healing disagreements that does no harm—it promotes healing. My credentials are: 1) I have common sense, and 2) I have a caring heart.

Self Talk for Healing Disagreements

Four things must be achieved to have a success-ful healing to a serious emotional disagreement:

1.   You must get your anger and frustration off your chest in a non-destructive way.

2.   You must calmly and rationally state your side of the argument as fairly as you can.

3.   You must calmly and rationally state the other person's side of the argument as fairly as you can.

4.   You must allow the healing to occur. There are two aspects to this, which will be dis-cussed shortly.

All of the above four things can be successfully achieved through self talk. Usually only one self talk session is needed. The example scenario I will give you shortly is a pattern for you to follow when you devise your own scenario for your own situation.

Setting the scene

You and your spouse are grocery shopping. As you wander through the crowded store together you make small talk about products and prices. You both agree that prices are way out of line and there doesn't seem to be any end in sight. You both wonder how you are going to be able to eat decently within your income if prices continue to increase.

You pick up a package of T-bone steaks to read the price out of curiosity.

Your spouse sees you and assumes you intend to purchase it and says in a loud, hostile tone that attracts the attention of all the other shoppers in the vicinity, "We can't afford that! If you didn't waste so damn much money on all those magazine subscriptions we could have steak! You can't have your magazines and steak too!"

At this point, you have several choices.

You can yell, "Screw you!" and stomp out of the store, thus laying the groundwork for a real nasty brawl shortly thereafter.

You can yell that your spouse wastes more money than you do and start itemizing each waste, thus escalating the moment into a full-scale war right there with plenty of spectators.

You can think to yourself, "Oops! This is one I had better handle later with self talk," and then put the steaks back with a soft, calm remark to your spouse, "Just price checking, not buying." You know something is festering in your spouse, but this is not the time or place to deal with it. You know you cannot ignore the situation because it is symptomatic of something. You are buying a little more time until you can be alone to handle the situation with self talk.

Here is a suggested self talk scenario for the situation I've just described. The portions in quotation marks are the words you would say out

loud to yourself. The other words are for information or explanation. This scenario is to be per-
formed while you are alone and cannot be
overheard by anyone.

The scenario

The first thing you need to do is get rid of your
anger and frustration

1. Yell or scream the words for this first step if
   you wish. Be emotional. Get it all out.

"What in the world is your problem
(spouse's name)? Today in the supermarket you
acted as though you didn't have the brains God
gave green apples! You embarrassed me and
humiliated me. Your behavior was totally unacceptable. I do not deserve that sort of verbal
abuse and you know it! You accused me of
wasting money on magazines. Well, I enjoy my
magazines and I have a right to some enjoyment. And what about you? You waste money .
. ." at this point go through the items (if any)
that you think are wasteful on your spouse's
part . . . "and I have never denied you anything
you enjoyed. Let's be fair about this . . ."

Continue to rant and rave out loud to
yourself until you have exhausted your anger.
Point out all the good things you have done.
Point out all the things your spouse has done

that annoy you. Let it all hang out in your own privacy.

When your anger and frustration are spent, you will have given yourself a much-needed, beneficial emotional cathartic. And no harm has been done.

At a subliminal level, your spouse's subconscious mind has received the message, but your spouse is not consciously aware of it. The subconscious mind does not deal in emotion, it deals only with information. This enables your spouse's mind to act on the information without rancor or bias, which is the first valuable step for successfully mending the disagreement.

2. Now clearly and calmly state your side of the situation out loud.

"I subscribe to (state the number) of magazines, which I read and enjoy. This costs approximately (state the cost) dollars a year, which certainly does not cripple us financially. In fact, some of the magazines nearly pay for themselves because they contain discount coupons which we use. I certainly have a right to have some magazines for my enjoyment. You are angry with me because of inflationary prices over which neither of us has any control, and that is just not fair. Perhaps you and I jointly need to restudy our entire budget and readjust our spending in all areas in a calm and mature manner. I am certainly willing to do this."

3. Now clearly and calmly state your spouse's side of the situation out loud, as fairly as you can.

"You are frustrated with the continuous rise in the cost of living that out-paces our income. You see my spending on magazines as a contributing factor to our financial stress. My magazines are ones you have no interest in, which probably is a factor in your frustration. You do have the right to question the wisdom of how we spend our money in all areas, including money spent on my magazines."

4. Now you allow the healing to begin. This involves two actions on your part. You must analyze the situation based on steps 2 and 3 above, and then state out loud your solution. Then you must take action based on your stated solution. In this specific example, you could have several different possible results of your analysis. Here are two sample self talk sessions dealing with different results:

(A) "I really am guilty of having too many subscriptions. I have eight subscriptions costing $175.00 a year. I rarely have time to read more than one or two, sometimes skimming the rest and sometimes not. I have stacks of back magazines that I intend to read someday and which currently take up all the floor space in two closets. I will cancel all my subscriptions except two and will discard all my back issues because I know I will never get around to reading them."

(B) "I do not have too many subscriptions. I have two that cost about $37.50 a year. This is reasonable. I do read and enjoy these magazines and I intend to continue them. I expect (state your spouse's name) to understand that his/her position is unreasonable in this matter."

Then you go and talk it over with your spouse, saying essentially either (A) or (B) above depending on which is the correct situation.

By the time you start talking to your spouse, the healing will have already made significant progress. Your healing is already 99% done.

Your spouse's healing is about 80–90% done due to the subliminal information received while you were doing your self talk. Your spouse will have already come to the same conclusion you have. Your discussion will merely be a formal crystallizing of your mutual opinions.

The outcome will be a stronger bond between you. The scenario I've given here is not likely to be your specific problem, but it is an excellent model for you to follow in resolving your specific problem.

To recap:

1. Purge yourself of anger and frustration.

2. State your side of the situation as accurately and fairly as you can.

3. State your spouse's side of the situation as accurately and fairly as you can.

4. Analyze steps 2 and 3 and adopt a solution.

5. Talk to your spouse about the solution.

Of course, all this must be done verbally (out loud) in order to gain the benefits of self talk that are discussed earlier in this book.

The power of this self talk approach is awesome. I can personally vouch for that. In my own experience I found that after you use it a few times for different situations, the serious spouse-related problems seem to cease completely, and you don't need to use the program again. It appears to have an all-encompassing influence on you and your spouse, to the extent that you seem to be able to avert problems before they become problems.

Formula For Success:
Mouth Power + Word Power = Personal Power

Chapter 14

Break a Leg!

(Self Talk to Overcome Stage Fright)

A decade or so ago the results of a nationwide survey were published, listing the ten top fears of adults in the United States of America. In the top ten were things like fear of death and fear of going to the dentist, neither of which seemed surprising.

But the #1 fear was a surprise. No one would have been likely to predict it. The #1 fear was "fear of standing up in front of a group of people and talking to them." Stage fright, if you will. Adults are petrified at the thought of addressing a group of people!

Public speaking is one of the most satisfying experiences one can have, yet no one wants to do it. They are afraid.

Because this fear is so widespread, I am writing this special chapter about it separate from Chapter 6, which deals with fears in general.

In 1962, I was earning a modest living as a technical writer trainee with IBM. It was readily apparent to me that I would probably retire in that same position unless I learned how to make myself more valuable to the company. It was also apparent from my observations that those who were moving up in the company were confident, outgoing people who could speak easily and authoritatively in a group.

I decided to turn myself into one of those people. I signed up for the Dale Carnegie Course in Public Speaking and Human Relations.

The course was one night a week for fourteen weeks, at four hours per night. One of the requirements was that each student had to speak in front of the class for two minutes, at least twice each night.

For the first speech on the first night, all we had to do was stand in front of the class and tell our name, what our occupation was, and some personal facts such as hobbies, until we filled the two-minute requirement.

One student was so petrified that he physically could not move his lips. In two minutes all he managed to do was mumble his name through sealed lips. The instructor asked him where he worked, and the hapless student could not remember. Later he told us that was the longest, most miserable two minutes he ever spent in his life. Fourteen weeks later, he was an articulate speaker, and loved public speaking.

Learning to speak in public was so beneficial to me that my entire career skyrocketed after completing the class.

Within four years I had advanced through three significant promotions: to Associate Writer to Senior Associate Writer to Department Manager. Within two years after that I advanced up two more levels of management to Project Manager to Development Manager.

That was just the beginning. Today I am a successful author of books and have many public speaking engagements. All of this occurred because I had learned how to speak to the public in 1962 and enjoyed doing it.

You also can have a similar success story to tell if you are willing to spend a few minutes a day performing the self talk scenario I will present in a few moments that will help you overcome stage fright and gain immense self confidence as a result.

The reason I devised this self talk program is because I realize that most of you do not have the opportunity to attend a professional public speaking class as I did. I make no pretense that this self talk exercise is a 100% substitute for the kind of intensive in-class training I received. My training went beyond public speaking to include human relations. For most of you, however, this self talk exercise will be sufficient to get you out of your shell and enable you to at least have the courage to stand up and say what you think in front of a group of people and feel good about yourself for having done it.

Self Talk for Public Speakers

The self talk scenario I will present shortly is to help prepare you mentally and emotionally for the experience of talking in front of a group of people. This scenario does *not* teach you how to talk—only actual experience can do that. In other words, self talk helps you get rid of your fear or apprehension, and to actually look forward to talking in front of a group. The actual doing is up to you.

Let's first consider some of the many opportunities to speak to groups that you could encounter in your everyday life:

1. At work in department meetings. You could be asked to give a presentation to the rest of the department concerning some aspect of your job. Or more commonly, you are a member of the group and you want to participate by asking questions or offering comments.

2. At PTA meetings, either as a leader or as an active group participant.

3. In politics. If you can talk in front of a group, you have a good chance of advancing in politics. Politicians will talk anytime, anywhere, at the drop of a hat. Unfortunately, many good speakers get elected based on their public speaking ability and they have nothing else to offer. You could change that by becoming active in politics, and having integrity and common sense to offer also.

4. Become a boy scout or girl scout leader.

5. Teach a Sunday school class.

6. Teach an adult education class.

7. Join an amateur theater group.

This list could be extended to be quite long. Nearly every person at sometime in his/her life has the opportunity to "give their two cents worth" in a group. Most people do not exercise this opportunity, preferring instead to keep their mouth shut. In their minds they have something important to say, but they have trouble getting their mouth to work.

The ones who open their mouths and speak are the ones who make things happen. They get what they want. They also gain the admiration of others. They also feel good about themselves.

The ones who have "lockjaw" don't make their ideas known. They usually do not get what they want. They don't make anything happen, and often they are the ones who complain in private about what is happening *to* them.

Scenario

There are two parts you need to do out loud. The first part you do only once. It is a two-minute speech in which you tell who you are and why you want to talk to groups of people.

The second part consists of some short statements that you must say daily for one month, then at least once a week thereafter until you become comfortable and confident with the idea of speaking in or to groups of people. You will know when the fear is gone.

Part 1: Shortly I will give you a sample script for a two-minute talk, as a pattern for you to follow. You will, of course, need to create your own script for your own situation.

The purpose of this self talk session is to clearly commit yourself to wanting to be able to speak in public. Without the commitment, there would be little value in repeating the affirmations in Part 2.

When you give your two-minute self talk speech I want you to stand up. The very act of doing this reinforces self-confidence. Stand tall and cast a long shadow—this creates a powerful self-image.

You have several options, all of which are good. Choose whichever one you wish.

1. Stand in front of a mirror and give the speech (out loud of course) to yourself.

2. Stand up and talk into an audio recorder, which you can then play back to hear yourself.

3. Have friends or family members be your audience, and you give your speech to them.

4. Have a friend capture you on video tape if you have a video camera available. Do not be concerned that you think you look terrible when you review the video. We all think we look terrible. Many professional actors and actresses refuse to view any of the movies they have appeared in for the same reason—they think they look terrible or sound terrible. These are human reactions and are normal.

Sample two minute script

"My name is Belinda Anderson, and until two months ago I was a household executive, a job I held for 20 years until my three children were grown. Now I need an outlet for my energies, so I have joined the workforce as a salesperson in the children's clothing department of the May Company.

When I applied for the job, the personnel manager said that I had no retail experience. I said yes I did, from the other side of the sales counter. I said I was an expert at buying clothes for boys and girls through the progression of all their ages, because I had reared two girls and one boy through all their ages. I knew what they liked and didn't like, and as a parent I knew the value of a dollar and of quality. I proposed that I well might be the most experienced person in children's retail that they had. I was hired on the spot.

Even though I am just starting out, I know I want to advance to department manager and even higher, perhaps to be a buyer or even store manager. To advance, I need to be able to present myself well verbally to strangers, executives, shoppers, groups of people. This is why I want to learn to overcome all apprehensions about public speaking and to learn to present myself verbally with confidence and ease. We have a storewide personnel meeting next month in which a corporate vice president will be present to discuss how we can increase sales and improve customer service. The vice president will be soliciting ideas from us. I already have some ideas, mostly from the customer viewpoint, that I want to be able to present effectively. So I intend to use self talk diligently to prepare myself for this important meeting and for what lies beyond that in my future. Thank you."

Now you prepare your own speech for your own situation. You may write it out if you wish. You may read it or memorize it, or speak extemporaneously, whatever is most comfortable for you. The important thing is to do it, thus committing yourself to a specific path of self-improvement.

Part 2: Here are some sample self talk statements to reinforce your speech in Part 1 and to condition your mind for public speaking. It is your choice where you say them—while driving, in the bathtub, while working in the yard, in front of a mirror, in front of friends, etc. Just do it daily, out loud. It only takes a minute or so.

"My thoughts and opinions are just as valuable as anyone else's. Sometimes my ideas are better than other people's."

"I have a strong desire to express my ideas in groups of people, and I shall do so at every opportunity."

"I am confident in my ability to express my ideas any time and any place."

"I have something worthwhile to say, and I shall say it with confidence."

The preceding statements are samples to get you started. Build on these samples to create your own tailored statements that suit your own needs.

The secret to success in this self talk is practice,persistence, and determination.

Self talk to overcome stage fright is especially powerful to use with family, friends, and co-workers. Since a great many people have this fear of public speaking, it is likely you know some people who also have this fear. Get a group together and each of you do self talk in the presence of the others. You will all benefit greatly. You could even expand to create more self talk speeches about various topics.

For example, pick a controversial topic such as abortion, gun control, pre-marital sex and so forth.

Then each of you can express your ideas in a two minute self talk.

One rule: There is to be no criticism. The only purpose is to give you each a forum for expressing yourself.

You can, of course, use self talk on various subjects out loud by yourself. You don't have to have others present. Keep in mind that what you are doing is training yourself to express your ideas out loud so that you will be able to do so in a real situation effectively.

If the PTA Chairperson asks, "Mr. or Mrs. Jones, what do you think about the school lunch program?" you want to be so conditioned by your self talk training to the point where you would immediately stand up, smile, and say, "I think . . ." and go on to confidently say what you think.

Break A Leg!, which is the title of this chapter, is a show business expression to wish a fellow performer good luck just before he/she goes on stage.

So I say to you with deep sincerity as you proceed in your efforts to overcome stage fright and become a good, confident public speaker—"BREAK A LEG!"

Formula For Success:
Mouth Power + Word Power = Personal Power

Chapter 15

This One Is for You, Hot Head

(Self Shout Temper Tantrums)

This chapter is a very important one because it can help you to protect your mental and physical health.

We live in a stressful society. Your job, your boss, your spouse, your kids, the IRS, the drive to and from work, the high cost of living, a death or illness, the government, mechanical malfunctions, a non-stop streak of foul weather, the postal service, the dentist, in-laws, blood relatives, too much exposure to loud or irritating noises, and a million more things are all sources of stress for you at any given moment.

Most of us can handle a certain amount of stress reasonably well—most of the time. Some of us have a very low stress tolerance. And all of us, at one time or another have a sufficient amount of stress placed on us that we buckle under—we want to explode—we stop functioning the way we normally function. We have stress overload.

If we have too much stress overload, too frequently, it can take a toll on our mental and physical health. We are in danger of becoming grouchy, negative, depressed, mentally ill in some form; we may develop a wide variety of physical ailments including a heart attack, or we may develop some socially unacceptable behavior such as becoming angry to the point of violence. Stress can literally cripple you in some way, or even kill you if not dealt with properly.

Consult your health practitioner concerning all aspects of stress and how to handle it. There is no intent in this book to give medical advice.

There is, however, a common-sense thing we can all do to help defuse stress before it builds up to become a problem.

Think of stress as being like steam pressure in a container. If the steam pressure continues to build up and there is no safety valve on the container, the steam will eventually explode the container, damaging it and anything nearby.

A common pressure cooker has a safety valve that will open up and release steam at a certain pressure. Often the pressure cooker will also have a backup fuse plug that will blow out if the regular safety valve doesn't open up when it should. We take care to design mechanical equipment with safety valves in order to prevent accidents.

But what about ourselves? What do we do to provide a safety valve for ourselves? Most people do nothing, and that is tragic because there are safety valves available. Your physician can advise you about some of them.

There is one safety valve available right now, for free, that doesn't need a prescription, that can serve as a safety valve for your stress pressure. The safety valve is a special self talk scenario that I will present to you shortly.

Typically, a person will deal with stress in either of two ways: 1. Hold it in. Try to be tough about it. Don't let anyone know how it is tearing you up inside. 2. Release it with no holds barred against anyone or anything you can get your hands on.

The first method can eventually harm your health or even kill you. The second method can cause property damage and physical harm to others, and land you on the wrong side of the law.

What needs to be done is to regularly release stress in a non-harmful way. That is what the following self talk scenario can do for you if you use it.

Scenario

The objective of this self talk session is to force yourself to let off steam. I sub-titled this chapter "Self Shout Temper Tantrums" because that is exactly what you must do. I want you to throw a tantrum. Do not merely talk—SHOUT. Get yourself worked up. Shout whatever comes to mind.

I will give you a mini-script just to give you the idea of what to do, but in actual practice you will not use a script, you will throw your tantrum extemporaneously. Wing it as you go along. Be eloquent. Swear. Whatever you choose.

You are also going to use physical violence in a healthy, harmless way.

Roll up some newspaper to form a paper club. You may want to put some tape or rubber bands around it to help hold it together because you are really going to abuse the paper club. You may want to have several paper clubs on hand so you can grab a fresh one after destroying one.

Next go somewhere private. Your garage. In a room with the door closed. In a field or forest. In the mountains. In a remote part of a city park. The idea is to be by yourself so you can shout and pound your paper club against something solid like a post, tree, sturdy table top, a rock, the floor—anything that the paper won't damage.

You are going to yell your frustrations while you punctuate your words by smashing your paper club as hard as you can against some obstacle that will eventually destroy your club.

Imagine that today you had a particularly high-pressure atmosphere at work. The drive home was terrible—a two-hour traffic jam in ninety-degree weather and no air conditioning in your car. Once home, a letter from the IRS informs you that you are being audited. You have had it! You have had enough of this crap!

You roll up and tape a newspaper and go to the garage. You stand in front of one of the exposed 2x4 support studs. You swing your club out gently to measure the distance and adjust your stance so when you swing the paper club you will land it solidly on the stud.

Then you throw your tantrum. It might go something like this: (SLAM indicates you swinging your paper club as hard as you can against the 2x4 support stud).

"I AM SICK (SLAM) AND FRIGGING (SLAM) TIRED OF THIS CRAP! (SLAM). THE I (SLAM) R (SLAM) S (SLAM) SHOULD BE CATCHING CROOKS (SLAM) INSTEAD OF PICKING (SLAM) ON US LAW-ABIDING (SLAM) CITIZENS (SLAM). MY JOB SUCKS (SLAM). IF HIGHWAY TAXES (SLAM) WERE USED PROPERLY (SLAM) WE WOULD NOT (SLAM) HAVE (SLAM) THIS DAMN (SLAM) TRAFFIC CONGESTION (SLAM)."

You get the idea. Be creative. Let it all hang out. Leave no stone unturned in your effort to release steam about everything that is annoying you. Nothing is sacred. Keep shouting and pounding the paper club until you feel you have said it all and you are too tired to continue.

Now you have released your stress in a beneficial way. Now you have rejoined the human race and are fit to be around. You feel better, because you are better. And looking back, it was fun. In fact, you had a great time getting rid of all that excess stress crap you had been carrying around bottled up inside you.

I recommend you throw one of these self shout temper tantrums often—perhaps daily if you feel the need. Perhaps once a week just to "clean house" and keep "tuned up."

I recommend one other thing. When you throw your tantrum have a copy of this book laying nearby. Then if someone should appear and wonder if you have gone bonkers, you can smile and show them the book, saying, "I'm just giving myself a stress-release tune up. It is all in this book."

Then they won't think you are crazy.

Instead, they will think that I am crazy.

Formula For Success:
Mouth Power + Word Power = Personal Power

Chapter 16

Warm Fuzzies

(Self Talk Self-Praise)

When someone compliments you on your appearance or behavior, or tells you that you have done a good job, or even gives you a big hug "just because," that is commonly called a Warm Fuzzy.

We all like to receive warm fuzzies, and we should all look for opportunities to give warm fuzzies to others. Praise is a powerful energy for good when used sincerely and judiciously. There is nothing more effective for healing a bruised ego or soothing a frayed spirit than an application of praise. Praise is marvelous for building strong, healthy self-esteem.

I remember the movies of a few years back where heroes and heroines were not allowed to accept praise. The tall, soft-spoken stranger would ride into town enroute to somewhere else. (In those

145

days, all heroes were tall, soft-spoken strangers who just rambled from place to place with no visible means of support).

Predictably, the town was held in the grip of fear by a host of at least a hundred bad guys. Of course, the tall, soft-spoken stranger took time out to clean up the town single-handedly before moving on to the next town.

Just before the tall, soft-spoken stranger mounted his horse to leave, the town's good people gathered around and tried to heap praise on him. But he wasn't allowed to accept praise. So he just looked down at the ground, kicked a stone with the toe of his boot, and softly said, "Shucks. It weren't nothin'," after which he rode off into the sunset.

I suppose this was to show that one should always be humble. I agree with that. We should be humble. But accepting praise does not make us lose our humility.

Bragging is not humble. Bragging is carrying self-praise to an unacceptable extreme. No one likes to be around a braggart.

I bet that after our tall, soft-spoken stranger rode far enough out of town where no one could hear him, he halted his horse and said out loud to himself (and to his horse), "You did a good job, Slim." And then he rode on to clean up the next town.

It takes a healthy self-esteem to tackle the problems we face every day and to always win over those problems. Self-esteem feeds on praise for nourishment, and more often than not there is no one who gives you that nourishment. Therefore, you must give it to yourself if you want to be a winner in life. **Self-praise is okay!** In fact, it is required for good self-esteem. Our tall, soft-spoken stranger knew that intuitively when he said out loud in private, "You did a good job, Slim."

So I encourage you to start today, and to continue every day for the rest of your life, to say out loud to yourself in private, "You did a good job, girl" or "You did a good job, guy." or some similar simple statement of self-praise.

That is all there is to self talk self-praise. It is simple, but extremely beneficial.

Self-praise

To those of you who are deeply indoctrinated into the "Shucks. It weren't nothin' " mode of thinking and are reluctant to switch to self talk self-praise, I offer the following for you to think about:

"Of all the people you will know in your entire lifetime, you are the only one you will never leave nor lose. To the problems of your life, you are the only solution. To the questions of your life, you are the only answer."

The above statement is pure truth. The message is clear. You must take care of you. You have full responsibility for yourself and your circumstances at all times.

So accept your responsibility now. Start feeding your self-esteem with self talk self-praise for a job well done.

You don't have to clear all the bad guys out of town before you deserve self-praise. In fact, rarely will you ever do something of that magnitude.

It is handling the little everyday situations that need self-praise because you almost never receive praise for them. A couple examples to give you the idea:

1. You are test driving your new car alone on a remote, little traveled country road and you get a flat tire. You have never changed a tire before in your life. You aren't even certain where the spare tire and tools are. It takes you over an hour, but you do manage to change the tire successfully. That certainly deserves a self talk self-praise, "You did a good job, (your name)."

2. You pull into a shopping center parking lot and notice a parked car with its lights on. You check the car door. If it is unlocked, you open the door and turn the lights off. If the door is locked, you write down the car description and license plate number, which you give to the information booth attendant inside the mall so an announcement can be made over the public address system. Give yourself self talk self-praise for this, "You did a good job, (your name)."

Everyday you have opportunities to give yourself self talk self-praise. You were patient with your children when you would rather have screamed at them. You refrained from telling someone off when you would rather have cussed them out. You kept going when you would rather have quit. You went straight home from work to be with your family, even when buddies wanted you to stop off for a couple hours of beer drinking. These are all excellent chances for self talk praise. You can easily come up with many more.

So do it starting now, and continue to do it— SELF TALK PRAISE.

To get you started, I say to you sincerely, "You did a good job, girl, for reading this book. You did a good job, guy, for reading this book."

Formula For Success:
Mouth Power + Word Power = Personal Power

Chapter 17

Look, Ma! No Hands!

(Opening Creative Channels with Self Talk)

Remember when you learned to ride a bicycle? Once you mastered basic balancing and riding, you branched out to learn to ride without holding onto the handle bars. When you achieved that, you rode by your house holding your hands above your head shouting, "Look, Ma! No hands!"

Then you were pleased with yourself so you didn't progress any further with a bicycle. You didn't learn to ride on the rear wheel while holding the front wheel high off the ground. You didn't learn to spin around on the rear wheel, or jump or dance with your bike. Your creativity stopped with "Look, Ma! No Hands!"

Riding with no hands is no big deal. Most everyone can do it. It requires a little creativity, but not much. Isn't that the way most of us go through life? We use a tiny bit of creativity—just enough to get by—and that is the end of it. No further progress.

What a shame! An infinite amount of creativity is available to all of us *if* we ask for it. In a moment I will show you how to ask with self talk.

The only essential difference between you and a genius is the genius has asked for more creativity and then uses it when he/she gets it. The conclusion is clear: Become more creative and you will become a genius.

Most people equate creativity with being an actor, a musician, a composer, an author, a painter, or a poet. These are certainly profound examples of creativity, but creativity encompasses much more than these endeavors.

Doing needlepoint is creative. So is woodworking, clothing design, gourmet cooking, and problem solving to mention just a few.

Whenever you extend your intelligence to cause something to become reality, you are creative. Probably the most common example of creativity is problem solving. For hundreds of years it was impossible to mass-produce clothing. Elias Howe studied the problem and then created the sewing machine as a solution.

Mulligan stew was probably created by some hobo who had a few odds and ends of various food. He was hungry, so he studied the problem and became creative.

Crafts are another expression of creativity that is quite common.

Every time you do something creative you become more of a quality person than you were before. That is just what creativity does for people. It brings out and reinforces the best in you. It doesn't make any difference whether you write a book, build a rocking chair, crochet an afghan, create a new casserole dish, or negotiate a peace treaty between two hostile nations. It is all creative, and you benefit personally for having done it.

Every one of us, without exception, has the ability to be more creative than we currently are. We have the ability to extend our intelligence to bring something into reality that doesn't currently exist.

Our subconscious mind, which is our obedient servant, will furnish us with whatever creativity we need or can handle. All we need to do is ask.

We ask, of course, using self talk out loud.

Self talk for creativity

Every book, article, and story that I have written was done in self talk consultation with my subconscious mind. By asking, I received and thus became more than I was before.

In the beginning, when I first started talking out loud to my subconscious mind, I had the concept that my subconscious was one intelligence source. I promptly named my subconscious "Clyde" and always addressed my self talk to Clyde. "Clyde, I have a problem," I would begin and then state what it was I wanted to do. I got help 100% of the time.

Over a period of time, Clyde revealed to me that he was not simply one intelligence source; that he, in fact, was seven distinct intelligence masters of my superconscious, with each master being responsible for a specific area of my mind and creativity. Among them, the seven masters covered every aspect of my life.

I now address these masters by name (I was given their names), sometimes individually and sometimes collectively, in my self talk.

Carl Weschcke, who is president of Llewellyn Publications, knew I used self talk so he wrote me a letter requesting I write a book about it—this book. At the time, I had no idea of what to write. So I asked my masters (my superconscious mind) for help, and they guided me through the creation of this book.

All this personal digression is to make a point— you can do the same thing that I do to become more creative. Using self talk, always out loud, ask your subconscious for help.

I suggest you start out this way: "I desire to talk directly with my subconscious mind on an ongoing basis from now on for the rest of my life. To make communication easier, I am naming my subconscious mind _____ (state any name you choose to call your subconscious mind; for illustration, I will use the name Ibis for your subconscious mind).

"Ibis, I need your help and want your help to open up all of my creative channels so I can do more and become a more fulfilled person. I want to be more creative. Help me, please."

After that initial speech, just talk to Ibis as often as you wish about anything you wish for the rest of your life. Just always start out by addressing your subconscious by name (i.e., "Ibis, I have come to consult with you") in order to establish a solid, direct communication line.

Then stand back and watch what happens in your life. You will be amazed.

Of course, when your subconscious mind gives you creative ideas and you ignore them and do nothing with them, the ideas will cease to be given to you—the old "cry wolf" syndrome. So be serious about this. When you ask, you will get, but then you must act upon it if you want to progress.

Now you know how to open up your creative channels using self talk. The ball is now in your court. It is up to you to let the game begin.

Formula For Success:
Mouth Power + Word Power = Personal Power

Chapter 18

Sex

(To Talk or Not to Talk)

I debated with myself, using self talk of course, about whether or not to include a chapter on sex. I finally decided "yes" for two reasons:

1. "Sex" sells everything from automobiles to microwave dinners, and I want this book to sell.

2. If I don't include a "sex" chapter, I will get dozens of letters asking "why not?"

People today are obsessed with sexual performance perhaps they always have been, but today they are blatantly obvious about it.

I've always been of the opinion that sex is something you **do**, not talk about. This opinion was reinforced by my observations when I was in the Air Force. The guys who talked about sex weren't performing, and vice-versa.

But the question that is no doubt on your mind is, "Can self talk help me improve my sexual performance?"

ANSWER: Probably, if you think your performance needs improving.

Scenario

Sorry. You are on your own for this one. I wrote this book to be enjoyed by people of all ages and all religious persuasions. If sexual performance is your problem, I feel confident that your fertile mind can devise an appropriate scenario. If you need to open up your creative channels to do this, re-read Chapter 17.

End of chapter.

Formula For Success:
Mouth Power + Word Power = Personal Power

Chapter 19

What to Do When You Don't Know What to Do

(Fill Time Constructively with Self Talk)

I am never completely idle, because I don't like being idle. By idle, I mean having absolutely nothing to play at, work at, read, study, plan, or watch. To me, idle means just hanging around waiting for something to happen to fill in time. I have no tolerance for "idle."

I have this one life to live, and I have no intention of wasting one moment in a vacuum waiting for something to happen. I believe in making things happen because that is what makes life exciting and fulfilling.

159

It wasn't always like this. Years ago, I had plenty of "hang around" time, which used to tire me out because doing nothing is a very tiresome pastime, probably due to the frustration of nothing.

Then I discovered how self talk could fill my time completely, enjoyably, and satisfyingly. I used self talk to find what to do when I didn't know what to do. I continue to use the same self talk technique after I finish writing a book and I don't know what to write next. It works every time for me.

The technique is simple. Think about what you would do if someone came to you, such as a son or daughter, and said, "I'm bored. I don't have anything to do."

You would help that person by asking questions that could lead to their finding something to do. The questions might be: Is your homework done? Is your room straightened? Do you have a book to read? How about writing a letter to Grandma? Why not phone Jack, maybe he can shoot some baskets with you. And so forth.

You do exactly the same thing with yourself to help yourself find something to do. You question yourself out loud and answer yourself out loud. It is surprising how quickly you come up with an answer.

You can solve problems the same way. An example scenario might go something like this (remember, all questioning and answering is to be done out loud):

Scenario #1

You are driving a truck on an unfamiliar narrow country road, due to a detour, and you approach an overpass labeled CLEARANCE 12' 11". You know your rig is slightly less than 13' 0" but you don't think it is a full inch less, so you brake to a stop. A quick visual glance tells you that you will tear the roof off the trailer if you try to go under the overpass.

Q: "Now what do I do?"
A: "I could turn around and go back to pick up some other route."

Q: "How am I going to do that? This narrow road has no shoulders and there is a deep ditch on each side."
A: "That's right. There is no way I can turn this rig around here.

Q: "Should I put out some flares and then hike to a telephone somewhere?"
A: "I could do that I suppose. Or maybe I could try to get someone on the CB."

Q: "Why not check closely to see exactly how much more clearance is needed?"
A: "OK." You then ease the rig up carefully so the front edge of the trailer is nearly touching the bottom of the overpass.

Q: "How much more clearance is needed?"
A: "About a quarter inch," you answer after sizing it up closely.

Q: "So why not lower the rig about a half inch by letting some air out of all the tires? I can refill the tires at the next service station I come to."
A: "Good idea."

You solved the problem by using self talk to repeatedly ask yourself questions and examining options. I realize this is a simplistic example, but it does effectively illustrate the process.

This process works to solve problems, to flush out fresh ideas, or to come up with something to do when you are bored and want something to do.

Self talk is always simple. You just meet the situation head on by talking it over with yourself. Ask simple, direct questions and give simple, direct answers, and you will lead yourself to exactly where you want to be.

Scenario #2

It is 2 p.m. You have one hour to kill before leaving for the airport to pick up your spouse.

Q: "What can I do for one hour?"
A: "Go to the airport early and hang around."

Q: "No. I want something constructive to do. Tell me what."

A: "Television, radio, or tapes would do it."

Q: "No. Try again."

A: "Read a book or magazine."

Q: "I've read the magazines already and there isn't enough time to start a book. Give me a one hour project, okay?"

A: "Write to your sister. You owe her a letter."

Q: "Hmm? Not a bad idea."

A: "You could mail it enroute to the airport."

Q: "Okay. I'll do it. Thanks."

You are probably wondering why you need to go through these conversations out loud. Couldn't you just do it silently in your head?

Yes, you could do it in your head, but you are less likely to get quick, solid results. This is because when you just think about these things, your mind easily gets distracted. You are quite likely to end up just having a rambling daydream session rather than achieving constructive results. Remember in an earlier chapter I discussed how your mind is like a recalcitrant child?

By actually talking out loud you focus intently on the situation and force an acceptable solution quickly.

It is easy to daydream non-productively for an hour, but it is difficult to talk out loud to yourself for an hour. The very nature of talking out loud to yourself forces results so you can stop talking. A little talk goes a long way.

Formula For Success:
Mouth Power + Word Power = Personal Power

Chapter 20

C'est la Vie

(Set Priorities Using Self Talk)

I have a friend who is a talented artist, but you wouldn't know it because he doesn't paint very often. He doesn't have time. Forty hours a week are spent earning a living at a mundane, non-artistic job. Then he has the usual things to do around the house: weeding and tending to the lawn, painting his sun-bleached house, the customary repair jobs like sticking doors and cracked tiles, and so forth.

Funny thing, he doesn't get around to the household chores either because he has so many other things to do and there are only twenty-four hours in a day, and he also does have to eat and sleep.

What other things? Most weekends there is a party or two. Always something to celebrate. And every weekday evening starting with the six o'clock television world news, straight through until 10:30

at the end of the local news, there are "must see" programs that absolutely cannot be missed. He does have time to do these things.

So there just isn't time to paint pictures, and he constantly bemoans it, "I love to paint, but I never seem to have the time."

I have said to his face, "That is a crock of (you know what). Every person on earth has twenty-four hours in a day—no more—no less. All the pictures ever painted, all the books ever written, all the inventions ever created were done by men and women who only have twenty-four hours in a day. So don't cry to me that `I don't have time'."

The truth is that we all can find time to do whatever it is we really and truly want to do. One secret to success is to make maximum use of your time and to learn to set, and stick to, priorities.

My wife crochets afghans while watching television and does needlework on long airplane rides—maximum use of time.

My friend *could* paint a picture a week if he wanted to badly enough. If a painting requires ten hours work, he could trade off two hours of television each night for five consecutive nights. It is just a matter of setting priorities and then sticking to them.

In this book I have already shown you how to make maximum use of your time by doing your self talk while taking a bath or driving your vehicle, and so forth.

Self talk can also help you set, and stick to, priorities if you have a problem similar to my artist friend.

The following sample self talk session is based on my artist friend's situation.

"I am going to paint a mountain scene this week which will take me about ten hours. I am determined to do this and I shall discipline myself to do it. I shall paint from 6 p.m. until 8 p.m. every evening until I am one hundred percent finished. No matter what is on television at that time, I will not watch it or listen to it. That is my painting time. If I feel like painting beyond 8 p.m., I shall. However, I will not stop painting until I have put in two full hours in each session. And I shall paint every day without fail until my picture is one hundred percent complete. I will not make excuses for not painting. I will paint because that is truly what I want to do. It is my number one priority."

Create a similar self talk session for whatever your particular priority problem is, and say it out loud daily until you have successfully made the priority a living part of your life so it is no longer a problem.

John Greenleaf Whittier (1807-1892) wrote:

For of all the sad words of tongue or pen,
The saddest are these: It might have been!

Don't let your life's story be one that "might have been." The way to change this potential sadness of "it might have been," into a living joy of

actual achievement in your life is to use self talk
daily to set, and execute, your priorities.

All the things in this chapter I have said to my
artist friend. Did it work for him? Well, no, because
he doesn't have time to do the self talk.

C'est la vie!

Formula For Success:
Mouth Power + Word Power = Personal Power

Chapter 21

A Different Drummer

(What Self Talk Can Mean for You)

Henry David Thoreau (1817-1862), the great American essayist and poet, once wrote:

> *If a man fails to keep pace with his*
> *companions,*
> *Perhaps it is because he hears a different*
> *drummer.*
> *Let him step to the music he hears,*
> *However measured or far away.*

Thoreau was wisely stating that people who make their own choices, who deliberately set out to determine their own destiny, who march to their own tune in life should be allowed—even encouraged—to do so. The implication is, and correctly so, that the world is a better place for having people who listen to, and follow, a different drummer.

He also wrote: "The masses of men lead lives of quiet desperation."

Here Thoreau was observing that most people deliberately lead unfulfilling, low achievement lives because they march to someone else's drummer rather than to their own drummer.

Self talk is a tool you can use to write your own music in life. It enables you to be your own drummer and march to your own tune.

It is that simple, and that powerful.

All you need to do is decide for yourself whether you want to "lead a life of quiet desperation" or to listen to a different drummer and march to that tune.

This book shows you one way to write your own tune by using self talk.

This book does not cover all the possibilities and potentials of self talk, but it is an excellent start. As you use self talk you will probably develop your own unique methods and purposes.

I would be delighted to hear from you concerning your self talk experiences. If you develop new uses, let me know. Perhaps I will be able to include them in a future edition of this book.

If I do include your contribution in a future edition be aware that:

1. You will not receive any compensation for it;

2. I will use your name *only* if you authorize me to do so in writing when you send me the contribution;

3. I will send you a personal reply *only* if you enclose a stamped, self-addressed return envelope. I think you understand why these three conditions are necessary.

You may write to me as follows:

William W. Hewitt
c/o Llewellyn Publications
P.O. Box 64383
St. Paul, MN 55164-0383

Llewellyn Publications will forward the letter to me.

Formula For Success:
Mouth Power + Word Power = Personal Power

Chapter 22

Grates Me the Sum

(My Hopes Regarding Self Talk)

Many decades ago when I was a senior in high school I took a competitive college scholarship examination. The test took all day, and some three hundred students participated. The top scorer would be awarded a full four-year scholarship to Bowling Green University in Ohio. The next nine would receive an Honorable Mention Certificate, but nothing else. Below the top ten, there would be no award of any kind.

One question on the exam was a heavily weighted two-part essay-type question. We had to identify the specific literary work that the sentence "Grates me the sum" came from and also interpret the meaning of the sentence.

I had no idea of the answer. It sounded to me like something Shakespeare might have written, but I had no idea which of his works or what the meaning might be. So I guessed one of Shake-speare's plays and guessed at a meaning.

My answer was not correct, and I had to settle for an Honorable Mention Certificate, which I threw away in anger at myself for not knowing the right answer. In those youthful days, I had not yet learned that one does not win 100% of the time.

Ever since then "Grates me the sum" has nagged at my mind. Would I have won the scholarship if I could have answered the question? I will never know.

What does it mean? The line fascinated me so much that I've wanted to use it in speaking or writing someday. I felt compelled (until now) to not use it though, because I didn't know what it meant.

Finally, throwing caution to the wind, I said the heck with trying to understand what the line is all about—I am going to use it anyway, and then I'll feel better because I will have accomplished my long desired goal.

That is why I titled this chapter "Grates Me The Sum." This may seem like a foolish whim to you. But is it really? Think about it a moment. First of all, I ventured to explore something that I didn't under-stand, and in so doing, I feel better about it. And secondly, some reader might know the meaning of the line and where it appears in literature, and will be kind enough to write to me in care of the pub-lisher to enlighten me. Then I will be completely ful-filled on this issue. And the reader who writes me the letter will have made a new friend (me) and will feel good about helping.

Don't we all go through life like this much of the time. We hesitate to explore something we don't understand. We prefer to remain conventional and not allow our behavior to say "the heck with it, I will do it anyway."

I am asking you to take this attitude concerning self talk. You don't really understand how or why self talk works, but isn't it worth a shot? Why not? The heck with always being conventional! For once, loosen up and do something just because you want to. Talk out loud to yourself. You will feel better about yourself. It is a kick!

I suppose I am somewhat of an expert on self talk, but I don't fully understand all aspects of it either. I just do it, and it works. I have a great time, and my life keeps getting better, better, and better.

We are multi-faceted beings, we humans. There are many aspects to our nature. We are emotional, rational, spiritual, materialistic, inter-personal, intra-personal, ambitious, lazy, hopeful, cautious, goal seeking, self-appreciating, self-depreciating, and on and on. In this book, I have provided a broad spectrum of self talk programs to cover many of the aspects of life that we all encounter.

- My hope is that there is something in here to help everyone.

- My hope is that you will get a good enough feel for self talk to be able to devise your own programs for situations that are not covered in this book.

- My hope is that you will say "the heck with it" and start using self talk every day, for your benefit.

- My hope is, also, that someone will write and tell me what "Grates me the sum" means and where it appears in literature.

Formula For Success:
Mouth Power + Word Power = Personal Power

Chapter 23

Now Shut Up!

(When to Stop Talking and Why)

For twenty-two chapters I have been encouraging you to shoot off your mouth—to talk, talk, and talk incessantly to yourself out loud.

Do you have to continue talking on the same subject forever? No, you do not.

Do you have to continue talking on the same subject until you achieve 100% results? No, you do not.

There comes a time when you should shut up, and in this brief chapter I will tell you when and why.

Law of Being

It all has to do with the **Law of Being.** The Law of Being is a universal law that states:

"Whatever happens to you, whatever comes to you, whatever surrounds you will be in accordance with your consciousness and nothing else. That whatever is in your consciousness shall happen, no matter who tries to stop it. And whatever is not in your consciousness cannot possibly happen."

The Law of Being is pure truth. Truth is always simple.

Paraphrased: What you put into your mind you get out of it. Conversely, nothing in, nothing out.

The whole purpose of self talk is to program into your consciousness exactly what you want there for various circumstances. Once you have it programmed in, it is there to stay unless you do other programming to cancel it or change it. Once it is in your consciousness, there is no need to continue to program the same material. It is in there, and it will make things happen at exactly the right time and in exactly the right way for your best interests.

Once you have the scenario programmed into your consciousness, it is time to shut up on that particular scenario. Then relax, release the matter to your higher mind for handling, and go on to something else.

There are times when you perform a scenario only once, and the results are immediate. An example is the release of frustration as described in Chapter 15. The frustrations have been recently entered into your mind, and with one emotional self shout session you remove the harmful effects of the frustrations. You will find that anytime you can make your self talk emotional you can cause deeper and faster programming, thus getting faster, more solid results. That is the way emotion effects the mind.

Other times you may have to use self talk for more extended periods before you have programmed your mind sufficiently. An example is to stop smoking as described in Chapter 9. The smoking habit has been deeply programmed into your mind over a long period. Therefore, it is likely that it will take some time and persistence in order to program your consciousness to become a non-smoker.

However, you do not necessarily have to achieve 100% results before you stop your self talk for a particular purpose. Once you feel you have programmed your mind sufficiently, stop talking and release the matter to your higher mind for results.

Sometimes you get results so fast that you know you have succeeded with your programming. You can just shut up at that point.

But how do you know when to shut up when results do not happen quickly? It is just something you know intuitively. If you don't get that intuitive "knowing" then keep up the self talk.

I programmed myself daily for years that I wanted to become a successful author of books. I had no rational reason to believe that I could, or should, write books. But that is what I wanted, so I used self talk for that purpose.

One day I had a quiet, confident awareness deep inside that my consciousness was permanently programmed. At that point I still had not written a book of any sort and had no idea what to write about. Yet I knew in my heart that it would happen.

I immediately shut up. I did not continue to use self talk to become an author of books because *I knew* that it was now in my consciousness and, therefore, it shall happen. It must happen, because that is the Law of Being.

So I relaxed, released my thoughts of being an author, and went on to do and think other things.

Once I had shut up and relaxed and released, things happened fast. Within two weeks the entire concept for a book "bombed" into my mind out of nowhere. I sat down at the keyboard and began to write. The words came almost faster than I could type. In thirty days I had written the complete manuscript, and the concept for a second book had already "bombed" into my mind. I immediately started writing the second book.

Both books, *Hypnosis* and *Beyond Hypnosis*, are quite successful. I am off and running as an author because it is in my consciousness.

There comes a time when you must shut up, relax, and let things happen.

I have told you when to shut up, and why.

Now I will shut up.

Formula For Success:
Mouth Power + Word Power = Personal Power

HYPNOSIS
A Power Program for Self-Improvement, Changing Your Life and Helping Others
by William W. Hewitt

There is no other hypnosis book on the market that has the depth, scope, and explicit detail as does this book. The exact and complete wording of dozens of hypnosis routines is given. Real case histories and examples are included for a broad spectrum of situations. Precise instructions for achieving self-hypnosis, the alpha state, and theta state are given. There are dozens of hypnotic suggestions given covering virtually any type of situation one might encounter. The book tells how to become a professional hypnotist. It tells how to become expert at self-hypnosis all by yourself without external help. And it even contains a short dissertation going "beyond hypnosis" into the realm of psychic phenomena. There is something of value here for nearly everyone.

This book details exactly how to gain all you want to enrich your life at every level. No matter how simple or how profound your goals, this book teaches you how to realize them. The book is not magic; it is a powerful key to unlock the magic within each of us.

0-87542-300-0, 192 pgs., 5-1/4 x 8, softcover   **$7.95**

BEYOND HYPNOSIS
A Program for Developing Your Psychic & Healing Powers
by William Hewitt

This book contains a complete system for using hypnosis to enter a beneficial altered state of consciousness in order to develop your psychic abilities. Here is a 30-day program (just 10 to 20 minutes per day is all it takes!) to release your psychic awareness and then hone it to a fine skill through a series of mental exercises that anyone can do!

Beyond Hypnosis lets you make positive changes in your life. You will find yourself doing things that you only dreamed about in the past, including easy and safe out-of-body travel and communication with spiritual, nonphysical entities. Speed up your learning and reading abilities and retain more of the information you study. A must for students of all kinds! *Beyond Hypnosis* shows you how to create your own reality, how to reshape your own life and the lives of others—and ultimately how to reshape the world and beyond what we call this world! This book will introduce you to a beneficial altered state of consciousness which is achieved by using your own natural abilities to control your mind. It is in this state where you will learn to expand your psychic abilities beyond belief!

0-87542-305-1, 240 pgs., 5-1/4 x 8, softcover   **$7.95**

Prices subject to change without notice.

BRIDGES TO SUCCESS & FULFILLMENT
Techniques to Discover & Release Your Potential
by William W. Hewitt
In the tradition of Dale Carnegie and Norman Vincent Peale, William Hewitt's latest book will make you stop and think seriously about yourself and your life. In his trademark easy-reading style, this former IBM executive and motivational trainer offers something new in self-improvement: A blend of traditional and non-traditional techniques for dealing successfully with the changes, choices and stresses of our time.

Whether you are going through a divorce, loss of a job, a mid-life crisis, or simply want to get more out of life, *Bridges to Success & Fulfillment* provides the tools to build a happier tomorrow. Explore your life purpose, choices, altered states of consciousness, self hypnosis, meditation, prayer, self-talk, spirituality, astrology, dreams, difficult people, death, stretching your mind, committees, suicide, even good old boy networks. Hewitt's gutsy, humorous and common-sense approach will inspire you to take charge of your life, work with your higher consciousness, and begin to set in motion a future that is successful beyond your wildest dreams!
0-87542-323-X, 224 pgs., 5-1/4 x 8, illus., photos $7.95

THE LLEWELLYN PRACTICAL GUIDE TO CREATIVE
VISUALIZATION: For the Fulfillment of Your Desires
by Denning & Phillips
All things you will ever want must have their start in your mind. The average person uses very little of the full creative power that is his, potentially. It's like the power locked in the atom—it's all there, but you have to learn to release it and apply it constructively.

IF YOU CAN SEE IT . . . in your Mind's Eye . . . you will have it! It's true: you can have whatever you want, but there are "laws" to mental creation that must be followed. The power of the mind is not limited to, nor limited by, the material world. *Creative Visualization* enables Man to reach beyond, into the invisible world of Astral and Spiritual Forces. Some people apply this innate power without actually knowing what they are doing, and achieve great success and happiness; most people, however, use this same power, again unknowingly, incorrectly, and experience bad luck, failure, or at best an unfulfilled life.

This book changes that. Through an easy series of step-by-step, progressive exercises, your mind is applied to bring desire into realization! Wealth, power, success, happiness even psychic powers . . . even what we call magickal power and spiritual attainment . . . all can be yours. You can easily develop this completely natural power, and correctly apply it, for your immediate and practical benefit.
0-87542-183-0, 294 pgs., 5-1/4 x 8, illus., softcover $8.95

BEYOND HYPNOSIS
A Program for Developing Your Psychic & Healing Powers
by William Hewitt

This book contains a complete system for using hypnosis to enter a beneficial altered state of consciousness in order to develop your psychic abilities. Here is a 30-day program (just 10 to 20 minutes per day is all it takes!) to release your psychic awareness and then hone it to a fine skill through a series of mental exercises that anyone can do!

Beyond Hypnosis lets you make positive changes in your life. You will find yourself doing things that you only dreamed about in the past, including easy and safe out-of-body travel and communication with spiritual, nonphysical entities. Speed up your learning and reading abilities and retain more of the information you study. A must for students of all kinds! *Beyond Hypnosis* shows you how to create your own reality, how to reshape your own life and the lives of others—and ultimately how to reshape the world and beyond what we call this world! This book will introduce you to a beneficial altered state of consciousness which is achieved by using your own natural abilities to control your mind. It is in this state where you will learn to expand your psychic abilities beyond belief!

0-87542-305-1, 240 pgs., 5-1/4 x 8, softcover   **$7.95**

HYPNOSIS
A Power Program for Self-Improvement, Changing Your Life and Helping Others
by William W. Hewitt

There is no other hypnosis book on the market that has the depth, scope, and explicit detail as does this book. The exact and complete wording of dozens of hypnosis routines is given. Real case histories and examples are included for a broad spectrum of situations. Precise instructions for achieving self-hypnosis, the alpha state, and theta state are given. There are dozens of hypnotic suggestions given covering virtually any type of situation one might encounter. The book tells how to become a professional hypnotist. It tells how to become expert at self-hypnosis all by yourself without external help. And it even contains a short dissertation going "beyond hypnosis" into the realm of psychic phenomena. There is something of value here for nearly everyone.

This book details exactly how to gain all you want to enrich your life at every level. No matter how simple or how profound your goals, this book teaches you how to realize them. The book is not magic; it is a powerful key to unlock the magic within each of us.

0-87542-300-0, 192 pgs., 5-1/4 x 8, softcover   **$7.95**

Prices subject to change without notice.

ASTROLOGY FOR BEGINNERS
An Easy Guide to Understanding & Interpreting Your Chart
by William Hewitt

Anyone who is interested in astrology will enjoy *Astrology for Beginners*. This book makes astrology easy and exciting by presenting all of the basics in an orderly sequence while focusing on the natal chart. Llewellyn even includes a coupon for a free computerized natal chart so you can begin interpretations almost immediately without complicated mathematics.

Astrology for Beginners covers all of the basics. Learn exactly what astrology is and how it works. Explore signs, planets, houses and aspects. Learn how to interpret a birth chart. Discover the meaning of transits, predictive astrology and progressions. Determine your horoscope chart in minutes without using math.

Whether you want to practice astrology for a hobby or aspire to become a professional astrologer, *Astrology for Beginners* is the book you need to get started on the right track.

0-87542-307-8, 288 pgs., 5-1/4 x 8, softcover **$7.95**

TEA LEAF READING
by William W. Hewitt

There may be more powerful methods of divination than tea leaf reading, but they also require heavy-duty commitment and disciplined training. Fun, lighthearted, and requiring very little discipline, tea leaf reading asks only of its practitioners an open mind and a spirit of adventure.

Just one cup of tea can give you a 12-month prophecy, or an answer to a specific question. It can also be used to examine the past. There is no regimen needed, no complicated rules to memorize. Simply read the instructions and look up the meanings of the symbols!

Tea Leaf Reading explains the how it works, how to prepare the cup for reading, how to analyze and read tea leaf symbols, how to interpret the symbols you see. It provides an extensive glossary of symbols with their meanings so you can begin interpretations immediately; it provides an index, with cross-references for quick location of the symbols in the glossary; and it has an appendix of crystals and metals that can aid you in reading tea leaves and in other pursuits.

0-87542-308-6, 240 pgs., mass market **$3.95**

THE SECRET WAY OF WONDER
Insights from the Silence
by Guy Finley
Introduction by Desi Arnaz, Jr.
Discover an inner world of wisdom and make miracles happen! Here is a simple yet deeply effective system of illuminating and eliminating the problems of inner mental and emotional life.

The Secret Way of Wonder is an interactive spiritual workbook, offering guided practice for self-study. It is about Awakening the Power of Wonder in yourself. A series of 60 "Wonders" (meditations on a variety of subjects: "The Wonder of Change," "The Wonder of Attachments," etc.) will stir you in an indescribable manner. This is a bold and bright new kind of book that gently leads us on a journey of Spiritual Alchemy where the journey itself is the destination . . . and the destination is our need to be spiritually whole men and women.

Most of all, you will find out through self investigation that we live in a friendly, intelligent and living universe that we can reach into and that can reach us.
0-87542-221-7, 192 pgs., 5-1/4 x 8, softcover $9.95

THE SECRET OF LETTING GO
by Guy Finley
Whether you need to let go of a painful heartache, a destructive habit, a frightening worry or a nagging discontent, *The Secret of Letting Go* shows you how to call upon your own hidden powers and how they can take you through and beyond any challenge or problem. This book reveals the secret source of a brand-new kind of inner strength.

In the light of your new and higher self-understanding, emotional difficulties such as loneliness, fear, anxiety and frustration fade into nothingness as you happily discover they never really existed in the first place.

With a foreword by Desi Arnaz Jr., and introduction by Dr. Jesse Freeland, *The Secret of Letting Go* is a pleasing balance of questions and answers, illustrative examples, truth tales, and stimulating dialogues that allow the reader to share in the exciting discoveries that lead up to lasting self-liberation.

This is a book for the discriminating, intelligent, and sensitive reader who is looking for *real* answers.
0-87542-223-3, 240 pgs., 5-1/4 x 8, softcover $9.95

Prices subject to change without notice.